iPad™
For Seniors
FOR
DUMMIES®

by Nancy Muir

WILEY

Wiley Publishing, Inc.

iPad™ For Seniors For Dummies®

Published by
Wiley Publishing, Inc.
111 River Street
Hoboken, NJ 07030-5774

www.wiley.com

Copyright © 2010 by Wiley Publishing, Inc., Indianapolis, Indiana

Published by Wiley Publishing, Inc., Indianapolis, Indiana

Published simultaneously in Canada

For general information on our other products and services, please contact our Customer Care Department within the U.S. at 877-762-2974, outside the U.S. at 317-572-3993, or fax 317-572-4002.

For technical support, please visit www.wiley.com/techsupport.

Wiley also publishes its books in a variety of electronic formats. Some content that appears in print may not be available in electronic books.

Library of Congress Control Number: 2010930375

ISBN: 978-0-470-88317-4

Manufactured in the United States of America

10 9 8 7 6 5 4 3 2 1

WILEY

About the Author

Nancy Muir is the author of over 50 books on technology and business topics. In addition to her writing work, Nancy runs a website on technology for seniors called TechSmartSenior.com and is the webmaster for UnderstandingNano.com. She writes a regular column on computers and the Internet on Retirenet.com. Prior to her writing career Nancy was a manager at several publishing companies, and a training manager at Symantec.

Dedication

To my wonderful husband, Earl, who not only stood in line at the Apple Store with me for an hour to pick up an iPad on April 3rd, but also helped me get up to speed on its features quickly. Thanks, honey — you're the best!

Author's Acknowledgments

I was lucky enough to have Blair Pottenger, the absolute best editor in the world, assigned to lead the team on this book. Blair, I couldn't have gotten through this rush schedule without you. Thanks also to Dennis Cohen for his able work as technical editor, and to Debbye Butler, the book's copy editor. Last but not least, thanks to Kyle Looper, Acquisitions Editor, for hiring me to write this book.

Publisher's Acknowledgments

We're proud of this book; please send us your comments at http://dummies.custhelp.com. For other comments, please contact our Customer Care Department within the U.S. at 877-762-2974, outside the U.S. at 317-572-3993, or fax 317-572-4002.

Some of the people who helped bring this book to market include the following:

Acquisitions and Editorial

Project Editor: Blair J. Pottenger

Acquisitions Editor: Kyle Looper

Copy Editor: Debbye Butler

Technical Editor: Dennis Cohen

Editorial Manager: Kevin Kirschner

Editorial Assistant: Amanda Graham

Sr. Editorial Assistant: Cherie Case

Cartoons: Rich Tennant
(www.the5thwave.com)

Composition Services

Project Coordinator: Kristie Rees

Layout and Graphics: Ashley Chamberlain, Nikki Gately

Proofreaders: Melissa Cossell, Cynthia Fields

Indexer: BIM Indexing & Proofreading Services

Special Help: Steve Arany, Kirk Bateman, Leah Cameron, Jay Kern, Kevin Kirschner, Clint Lahnen, Kristie Rees, Bob Woerner

Publishing and Editorial for Technology Dummies

Richard Swadley, Vice President and Executive Group Publisher

Andy Cummings, Vice President and Publisher

Mary Bednarek, Executive Acquisitions Director

Mary C. Corder, Editorial Director

Publishing for Consumer Dummies

Diane Graves Steele, Vice President and Publisher

Composition Services

Debbie Stailey, Director of Composition Services

Table of Contents

Introduction

*I*f you bought this book (or are even thinking about buying it), you've probably already made the decision to buy an iPad. The iPad is set up to be simple to use, but still, it can take hours to explore the pre-installed apps, learn how to make settings, and sync it to your computer. I've put in those hours so you don't have to, and I've added advice and tips for getting the most out of your iPad.

This book helps you get going with iPad quickly and painlessly so you can get right to the fun part.

About This Book

This book is specifically written for mature people like you, folks who are relatively new to using computing gadgets and want to discover the basics of buying an iPad, working with the pre-installed apps, and getting on the Internet. In writing this book, I've tried to take into account the types of activities that might interest someone who is 50 years or older and is picking up an iPad for the first time.

Conventions used in this book

This book uses certain conventions to help you find your way around, including:

➡ When you have to type something in a text box, I put it in **bold** type. Whenever I mention a Web site address, I put it in another font, `like this`. Figure references are also in bold, to help you find them.

➡ Callouts for figures draw your attention to an action you need to perform. In some cases, points of interest in a figure might be indicated. The text tells you what to look for; the callout line makes it easy to find.

 Tip icons point out insights or helpful suggestions related to tasks in the step lists.

Foolish Assumptions

This book is organized by sets of tasks. These tasks start from the very beginning, assuming you've never laid your hands on an iPad, and guide you through from the most basic steps in non-technical language.

This book covers both Wi-Fi and Wi-Fi/3G iPad features. I'm also assuming you'll want to download and use the iBooks eReader app, so I tell you how to do that in Chapter 8 and cover its feature set in Chapter 9.

Why You Need This Book

The iPad is cool and perfect for many seniors because it provides a very simple, intuitive interface for doing things like checking e-mail and playing music. But why should you stumble around trying to figure out its features? With the simple step-by-step approach of this book, you can get up to speed with iPad right away and overcome any technophobia you might have.

You can work through this book from beginning to end or simply open up a chapter to solve a problem or help you learn a specific new skill whenever you need it. The steps in each task get you where you want to go quickly, without a lot of technical explanation. In no time, you'll start picking up the skills you need to become a confident iPad user.

How This Book Is Organized

This book is conveniently divided into several handy parts to help you find what you need.

➡ **Part I: Making the iPad Your Pad:** If you need to buy your iPad or get started with the basics of using it, this part is for you. These chapters help you explore the different specifications, styles, and price ranges for iPads and discover how to set up your iPad out of the box, including getting an iTunes account to buy entertainment content and/or additional apps. These chapters provide information for exploring the iPad Home screen when you first turn it on, and useful accessibility features to help out if you have hearing or vision challenges.

Part II: Taking the Leap Online: Here's where you find out how to connect to the Internet and use the built-in Safari browser. You putter with the pre-installed Mail app and set iPad up to access e-mail from your existing e-mail accounts. This is also the part where you get to shop online for multimedia content such as movies and music, and additional fun iPad apps.

Part III: Having Fun and Consuming Media: The iPad has been called essentially a device for consuming media such as music, podcasts, and movies. Built into iPad are an iPod app for playing music and the Videos and YouTube apps for watching video content. In addition, this is the part where I explain how to download and use iBooks, a free eReader app from Apple, and show you how to play around with the Maps app to find your favorite restaurant or bookstore with ease.

Part IV: Managing Your Life and Your iPad: For the organizational part of your brain, iPad makes available Calendar, Contacts, and Notes apps, all of which are covered in this part. I also offer advice about keeping your iPad safe and troubleshooting common problems that you might encounter.

Get Going!

Whether you need to start from square one and buy yourself an iPad or you're ready to just start enjoying the tools and toys your new gadget makes available, it's time to get going, get online, and get iPad savvy.

Part I
Making the iPad Your Pad

The 5th Wave   By Rich Tennant

"Other than this little glitch with the landscape view, I really love my iPad."

Buying Your iPad

You've read about it. You've seen on the news the lines at Apple Stores on the day it was released. You're so intrigued that you've decided to get your own iPad to have fun, explore the online world, read e-books, organize your photos, and more.

Trust me; you've made a good decision because the iPad does redefine the computing experience in an exciting new way. It's also an absolutely perfect fit for many seniors.

So, where do you begin?

In this chapter, you discover the different types of iPad models and their advantages, as well as where to buy this little gem. Once you've got one in your hands, I help you explore what's in the box and get an overview of the little buttons and slots you'll encounter — luckily, there are very few of them.

Choose the Right iPad for You

iPads don't come in different colors or sizes. In fact, if you pick up an iPad (see **Figure 1-1**) you're not likely to be able to tell one model from another. That's because the differences are pretty much under the hood.

Figure 1-1

There are two variations in iPad models:

 The amount of memory built into the iPad

 How you connect to the Internet: Will you just use Wi-Fi or will you use Wi-Fi and 3G

Confused? Read on as I explain the two variations in more detail in the following sections.

Decide How Much Memory Is Enough

Memory affects how much you can store on a computing device (for example, how many movies, photos, and applications you can keep there). Memory can also affect your iPad's performance when handling tasks such as streaming your favorite TV show from the Web or downloading music.

Streaming refers to watching video content from the Web, rather than playing a file located on your computing device. You can enjoy a lot of content online without ever downloading the full content to your hard drive, and given the iPad has a relatively small amount of memory in any of its models, that's not a bad idea. See Chapters 10 and 12 for more about getting your music and movies online.

So what are the memory options with an iPad? You can get 16, 32, or 64 gigabytes of memory in your iPad. It's important to choose the right amount of memory because you can't open the unit up and add memory as you can with a desktop computer. You also can't slot in a flash drive (also known as a USB stick) to add backup capacity because there is no USB port . . . or CD/DVD drive, for that matter.

So how much memory is enough for you? Here's a rule of thumb: If you like lots of media such as movies and photos or e-books and you want to store them on your iPad (as opposed to experiencing or accessing this content online on sites such as Hulu or Netflix), you might need 64 gigabytes. For most people who manage a reasonable amount of photos, download some music, but watch heavy-duty media like movies online, 32 gigabytes is probably sufficient. If you pretty much want to check e-mail, browse the Web, and make short notes to yourself, 16 gigabytes *might* be enough.

 Do you have a clue how big a gigabyte is? Consider this: Just about any computer you buy today comes with a minimum of 250 gigabytes of memory. Computers have to tackle larger tasks than an iPad so that makes sense. The iPad is, to a great extent, meant to help you experience online media and e-mail. Still, in the world of memory, 16 gigabytes is pretty puny.

What's the price for larger memory? In the first generation of iPad, a 16-gigabyte Wi-Fi unit (see the next section for more about Wi-Fi) will cost you $499; 32 gigabytes jump to $599; and 64 gigabytes add another $100, putting you back a whopping $699.

Determine if You Need Wi-Fi Only or Wi-Fi and 3G

Because the iPad is great for browsing online, shopping online, e-mailing, and so on, having an Internet connection for it is pretty important. That's where Wi-Fi and 3G come in. Both are technologies used to connect to the Internet. *Wi-Fi* is what you use to connect to a home network or your local coffee shop network. It's a network that has a reasonably limited range. If you leave home or walk out of the coffee shop, you can't get online (though some towns are installing town-wide Wi-Fi networks).

3G is a cell phone technology that allows an iPad to connect to the Internet via a cellular network that is widespread, just as you can make calls from just about anywhere using your cell phone.

You can buy an iPad with only Wi-Fi or one with both Wi-Fi and 3G. Getting a 3G iPad will cost you an additional $130 (see **Table 1-1**), but it also includes GPS so you can get driving directions. Also, to use your 3G network you have to pay AT&T a monthly fee. The good news is that there is no long-term contract as there is with your cell phone for a data connection — you can pay for a connection the month you visit your grandkids and then get rid of it when you arrive home. The bad news is that it could cost you $30 a month for unlimited access, or $15 a month for 250 megabytes of data (which is not a lot, trust me).

Table 1-1	iPad Models and Pricing	
Memory	*Wi-Fi*	*Wi-Fi and 3G*
16 GB	$499	$629
32 GB	$599	$729
64 GB	$699	$829

So how do you choose? If you want to wander around the woods or town with your iPad constantly connected to the Internet, get 3G and pay the price. But if you'll use your iPad mainly at home or in a location which is a Wi-Fi *hotspot* (a location where Wi-Fi access to the Internet is available), don't bother. And frankly, today, there are *lots* of hotspots out there, including restaurants, hotels, airports, and more.

The 3G iPad is a GPS device, meaning that it knows where you are and can act as a navigation system to get you from here to there. The Wi-Fi–only model uses a digital compass and triangulation method for locating your current position, which is much less accurate; with no constant Internet connection, it also isn't much use driving around town. If getting directions is one of the features of iPad that excites you, get 3G and then see Chapter 13 for more about the Maps feature.

Know Where to Buy Your iPad

Apple doesn't offer iPad through every major retail store such as Sears or through all major online retailers such as Newegg or Amazon. As of this writing you can buy an iPad at the Apple Store and through a few brick and mortar stores such as BestBuy, and at online sites such as MacMall.com.

If you get your iPad from Apple, either at one of their retail stores, or through their online store, here's the difference in the buying experience:

The Apple Store advantage is that the sales staff will help you unpack your iPad and make sure it's working properly, register the device (which you have to do before you can use it; see Chapter 2 for more about this process), and help you learn the basics of using it. On the day it launched there were workshops to help people learn about iPads, but even after the hoopla is over, Apple employees are famous for being helpful to customers.

However, Apple Stores aren't on every corner, so if visiting one isn't an option (or you just prefer to go it alone), you can go to Apple Store's Web site (`http://store.apple.com/us/browse/home/shop_ipad/family/ipad`), shown in **Figure 1-2,** and order one to be shipped to you. Shipping typically is free, and if there's a problem, Apple's online store customer service reps are also known for being very helpful and will help you solve the problem or replace your iPad.

Figure 1-2

Consider iPad Accessories

At present, Apple offers a few accessories you might want to check out when you purchase your iPad (or purchase later on down the road), including:

➡ **iPad Case:** Your iPad isn't cheap and, unlike a laptop computer, it has an exposed screen that can be damaged if you drop or scratch it. Investing in the iPad Case is a good idea if you intend to ever take your iPad out of your house — or if you have a cat or grandchildren. Currently, the case that Apple sells costs about $40.

➡ **iPad Camera Connection Kit:** Because there's no USB port on an iPad, the only way to upload photos from your digital camera is by sending them to your computer and then syncing them to the iPad (a process you hear more about in Chapter 3). This handy kit allows you to download digital photos directly to your iPad. It will set you back about $30 for the privilege.

⟼ **iPad Dock:** The iPad is light and thin, which is great, but holding it all the time can get tedious. The iPad Dock (see **Figure 1-3**) lets you prop it up so you can view it hands-free and charge the battery and sync to your computer. At about $30, it's a good investment for ease and comfort.

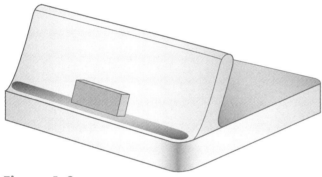

Figure 1-3

⟼ **iPad Keyboard Dock:** The iPad provides an on-screen keyboard that's passable, especially if you position it to view things in *landscape* orientation (that is, with the long side across the top). However, if you're a touch typist who wants to write long notes or e-mails, or you have larger hands and have trouble with the virtual keys on the screen, the iPad Keyboard Dock (see **Figure 1-4**) or a wireless keyboard might be the answer. The Apple accessory costs about $70.

Figure 1-4

➡ **iPad 10W USB Power Adapter:** This accessory is
    similar to the 10W USB Power Adapter that ships
    with the iPad. However, this accessory makes charg-
    ing easier if you need to place your iPad a bit further
    from a power outlet because this adapter sports a six-
    foot-long cord.

 There are already several companies producing iPad
    accessories such as cases, and more will pop up all
    the time, so feel free to search for different items and
    prices. iPad also supports Bluetooth, a technology
    that lets you connect with nearby Bluetooth-enabled
    devices such as wireless keyboards, so consider that
    an option to the Apple-offered iPad Keyboard Dock.

Don't bother buying a wireless mouse to connect
    with your iPad via Bluetooth — the iPad recognizes
    your finger as its primary input device, and mice
    need not apply.

Explore What's in the Box

When you fork over your hard-earned money for your iPad, you'll be left holding one box about the size of a package of copy paper. Here's what you'll find when you take off the shrink-wrap and open the box:

➡ **iPad:** Your iPad is covered in a thick plastic sleeve thingie you can take off and toss (unless you think there's a chance you'll return it, in which case you might want to keep all packaging for 14 days — Apple's return period).

➡ **Documentation (and I use the term loosely):** You'll find a small white envelope under the iPad itself about the size of a half-dozen index cards. Open it up and you'll find:

  • *A tiny pamphlet:* This pamphlet, named Important Product Information Guide, is essentially small print (that you mostly don't need to read) from folks like the FCC.

  • *A label sheet:* This contains two white Apple logos on it (not sure what they're for, but my husband and I use one of these stickers to differentiate my iPad from his).

  • *A small card:* This displays a picture of the iPad and callouts to its buttons on one side, and the other side contains about 3 sentences of instructions for setting it up and info about where to go to find out more.

➡ **Dock Connector to USB Cable:** Use this cord (see **Figure 1-5**) to connect the iPad to your computer, or use it with the last item in the box, which is . . .

➠ **10W USB Power Adapter:** The power adapter (refer to **Figure** 1-5) attaches to the dock connector cord so you can plug it into the wall and charge the battery.

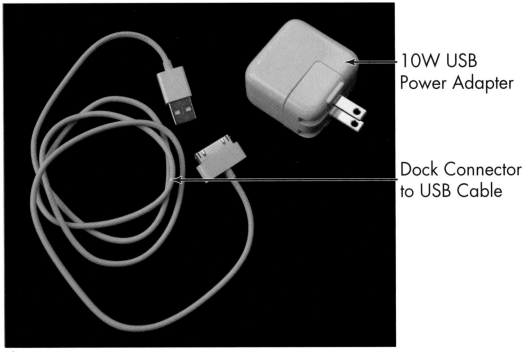

10W USB
Power Adapter

Dock Connector
to USB Cable

Figure 1-5

That's it. That's all there is in the box. It's kind of a study in Zen-like simplicity.

Take a First Look at the Gadget

The little card contained in the documentation (see the preceding section) gives you a picture of the iPad with callouts to the buttons you'll find on it. In this section, I give you a bit more information about those buttons and some other physical features of the iPad. **Figure 1-6** shows you where each of these items is located.

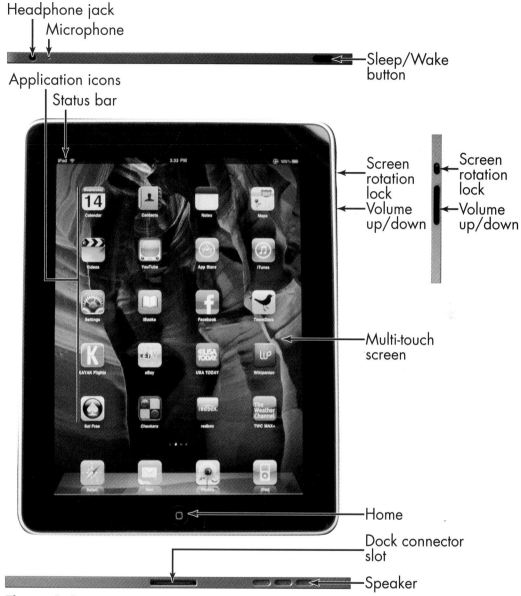

Headphone jack
Microphone
Sleep/Wake button
Application icons
Status bar
Screen rotation lock
Screen rotation lock
Volume up/down
Volume up/down
Multi-touch screen
Home
Dock connector slot
Speaker

Figure 1-6

Here's the rundown on what these things are and what they do:

◼▶ **(The all-important) Home button:** On the iPad, you go back to the home screen to do just about anything. If you're browsing online and you want to open the calendar, push the Home button and you exit the Web browser and end up on the home screen where you can open the calendar app. No matter where you are or what you're doing, push Home and you're back to home base.

➡ **Sleep/Wake button:** You can use this button (whose functionality I cover in more detail in Chapter 2) to power up your iPad, put it in sleep mode, wake it up, or power it down.

➡ **Dock connector slot:** This is where you plug in the dock connector cord to charge your battery or sync with your computer (which you learn more about in Chapter 3).

➡ **Screen Rotation Lock:** In case you hadn't heard, the iPad screen rotates to match the angle you're holding it at. If you want to stick with one orientation even if you spin the iPad in circles, you can use this little switch to lock the screen, which is especially handy when reading an eBook.

➡ **(A tiny, mighty) Speaker:** One of the nice surprises I had when I first got my iPad is what a great little sound system it has and how much sound can come out of this tiny speaker. The speaker is located on the bottom edge of the screen below the Home button.

➡ **Volume:** A volume rocker you tap up for more volume and down for less.

➡ **Headphone jack and Microphone:** If you want to listen to your music in private, you can plug a 3.5mm minijack headphone in here (including an iPhone headset if you have one, which gives you bidirectional sound). There's also a tiny microphone that makes it possible to speak into your iPad to do things like making phone calls using Internet calling services.

Looking Over the Home Screen

1 won't kid you: You have a slight learning curve ahead of you because iPad is different from other computers you may have used (though if you own an iPhone or iPod Touch, you've got a head start). That's mainly because of the multi-touch screen and on-screen keyboard, and the fact that you can't use a mouse with iPad. It doesn't have an operating system such as Windows or the Mac OS: What it does have is a modified iPhone operating system, so some of the methods you've used before (such as right-clicking) don't really work with the touchscreen.

Getting used to doing things with your fingers onscreen takes a little bit of time if you're used to using a mouse, but with patience, you'll find it's a very intuitive way to communicate with your computing device.

In this chapter, you turn on your iPad and register it and take your first look at the Home screen. You also practice using various methods of interacting with the touchscreen and get an overview of built-in applications.

Get ready to . . .

Have a soft cloth like one you use to clean your eyeglasses handy. You're about to deposit a ton of fingerprints on your iPad — one downside of a touchscreen device.

What You Need to Use iPad

At a bare minimum, you need to be able to connect to the Internet to take advantage of most of iPad's features. It's also helpful to have a computer to allow you to download photos, music, or applications from non-Apple online stores and transfer them to your iPad through a process called *syncing*. You also need a computer to register your iPad the first time you start it, although you can have the folks at the Apple Store handle that for you.

Can you use iPad without owning a computer and just using public Wi-Fi hotspots to go online (or a 3G connection if you have a 3G model)? Yes. However, to get the most out of a Wi-Fi–only iPad and use many of its built-in features, you should have a computer and home Wi-Fi network available.

Apple's iPad User Guide recommends that you have

→ a Mac or a PC with a USB 2.0 port and one of the following operating systems:

- Mac OS X version 10.5.8 or later

- Windows 7, Windows Vista, or Windows XP Home or Professional with Service Pack 3 or later

→ iTunes 9.1 or later, available at www.itunes.com/download

⟹ an iTunes Store account

⟹ Internet access

Apple has set up its iTunes software to help you manage content for your iPad, including movies, music, or photos you've downloaded, as well as where to transfer your calendar and contact information from. Chapter 3 covers those settings in more detail.

Turn iPad On and Register It

1. The first time you turn on your iPad you have to register it using a connection to a computer with the latest version of iTunes installed. Hold the iPad with one hand on either side, oriented like a pad of paper.

2. Press and hold the Sleep/Wake button on the top of your iPad until the Apple logo appears. In another moment, a screen appears showing a picture of a cord plugging into an iPad, indicating your next step.

3. Plug the Dock Connector to USB Cable into your iPad.

4. Plug the other end into a USB port on a computer. Both your computer and iPad think for a few moments while they exchange some data.

5. Sign in to your iTunes account in the dialog that appears, and then follow the simple on-screen instructions to register your iPad and choose what content is automatically downloaded when you connect your iPad to your computer. (You can change these settings later; this is covered in Chapter 3.) When you're done, your iPad Home screen appears and you're in business.

6. Unplug the Dock Connector to USB Cable.

 If you buy your iPad at an Apple Store, they'll register it for you and you can skip this whole process.

 You can choose to have the following transferred to your iPad from your computer when you sync: music, videos, downloaded applications, contacts, calendars, e-books, podcasts, and browser book-marks. You can also transfer content you download directly to your iPad using the iTunes and App Store features to your computer. See Chapters 7 and 8 for more about these features.

Meet the Multi-Touch Screen

When your Home screen appears (see **Figure 2-1**), you'll see a pretty picture in the background and two sets of icons. One set appears in the Dock along the bottom of the screen. The *Dock* contains the Safari browser, Mail, Photos, and iPod app buttons by default, though you can add other apps to it. The Dock also appears on every Home screen (adding new apps creates additional Home screens). Other icons appear above the Dock and are closer to the top of the screen. (I cover all these icons in the "Take Inventory of Built-in Applications" section, later in this chapter). Different icons appear in this area on each Home screen.

 This may or may not need saying, but the screen is made of glass and will smudge when you touch it and break if you throw it at the wall. So, be careful and treat it nicely.

The Dock

Application icons

Figure 2-1

The iPad uses a *touchscreen technology*, which means that when you swipe your finger across the screen or tap an icon, you're providing input to the device. You hear more about that in the next task, but for now, go ahead and play with it for a few minutes — really, you can't hurt anything. Use the pads of your fingertips (not fingernails) and do the following:

1. Tap the Settings icon. The various settings (which you hear more about in Chapter 17) appear (see **Figure 2-2**).

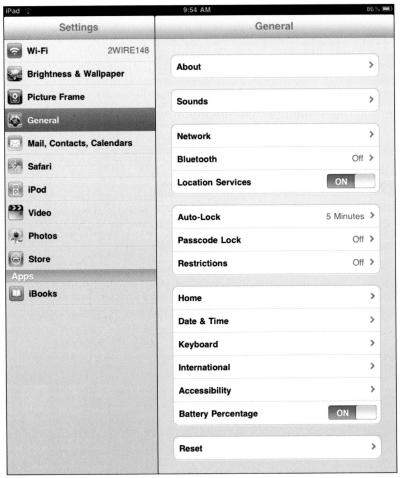

Figure 2-2

2. To return to the Home screen, press the Home button.

3. Swipe a finger or two from right to left on the screen. Because the iPad has a few additional Home screens available (11 to be exact) that you can fill up with all the applications you'll be downloading, the screen shifts slightly to the left. (If you had more apps downloaded filling additional Home screens, this action moves you to the next Home screen.) Also, with multiple Home screens in use, you get little dots at the bottom of the screen above the Dock icons, indicating which of the Home screens you're on.

4. To experience the rotating screen feature, while holding the iPad firmly, turn it sideways. The screen flips to a horizontal orientation. To flip it back, just turn the device so it's oriented like a pad of paper again.

 You can customize the Home screen by changing the background picture, called *wallpaper*, and changing the brightness. You can read about making these changes in Chapter 4.

Goodbye Click-and-Drag, Hello Tap-and-Swipe

There are several methods you can use for getting around and getting things done in iPad using its multi-touchscreen, including:

➡ **Tap once:** To open an application on the Home screen, choose a field such as a search box, select an item in a list, select a backward arrow to move back one screen, or follow an online link, tap the item once with your finger.

➡ **Tap twice:** Use this method to enlarge or reduce the display of a Web page (see Chapter 5 for more about using the Web browser, called *Safari*) or zoom in or out in the Maps app.

➡ **Pinch:** As an alternative to the tap-twice method, you can pinch your fingers together or move them apart on the screen (see **Figure 2-3**) when you're looking at photos, maps, Web pages, or e-mail messages to quickly reduce or enlarge them, respectively.

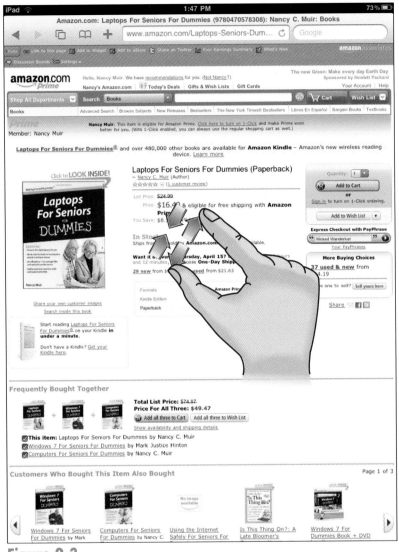

Figure 2-3

 You can use a three-finger tap to zoom your screen to be even larger. This is handy if you have vision challenges. Go to Chapter 4 to discover how to turn this feature on using Accessibility features.

➥ **Drag to scroll (also referred to as *swiping*):** When you press your finger to the screen and drag to the right, left, up, or down, you move around the screen (see **Figure** 2-4). Swiping to the right on the Home screen moves you to the Spotlight screen, Apple's term for the iPad search screen, for example. Swiping down while reading an online newspaper moves you down the page, while swiping up moves you back up the page.

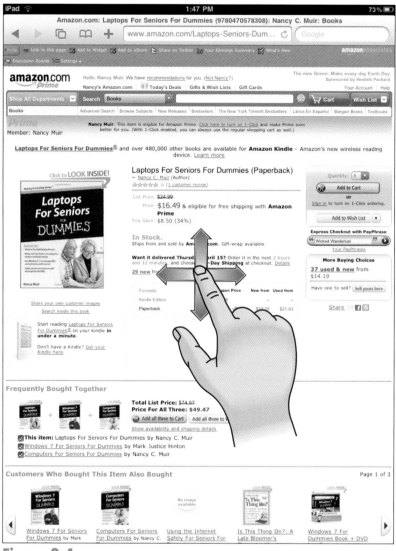

Figure 2-4

⟶ **Flick:** To scroll more quickly on a page, quickly flick your finger on the screen in the direction you want to move.

⟶ **Tap the Status bar:** To move quickly to the top of a list, Web page, or e-mail message, tap the Status bar at the top of the iPad screen.

⟶ **Press and hold:** If you're in any application where selecting text would be an option, such as Notes or Mail, or if you're on a Web page, pressing and holding near text will select a word and bring up editing tools that allow you to select, cut, or copy text.

Try these methods now by following these steps:

1. Tap the Safari button to display the Web browser. (You may be asked to enter your network password to access the network).

2. Tap a link to move to another page.

3. Double-tap the page to enlarge it; then double-tap again to reduce its size.

4. Drag one finger around the page to scroll.

5. Flick your finger quickly on the page to scroll more quickly.

6. Press and hold your finger down next to text that isn't a link. The item is selected and a Copy tool is displayed, as shown in **Figure 2-5.** (This one is tricky so if you don't get it right, don't worry! I cover text editing in more detail in Chapter 16.)

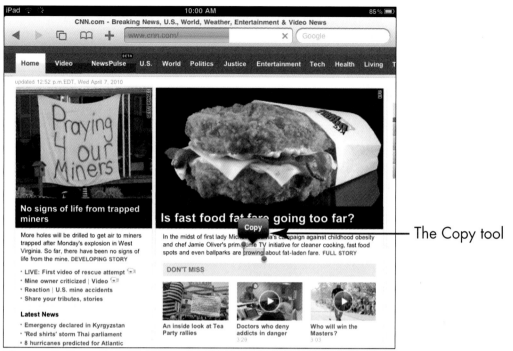

The Copy tool

Figure 2-5

7. Press and hold your finger on a link or an image. A menu appears with commands that allow you to open the link or picture, open it in a new page, or copy it. The image menu also offers a Save Image command.

8. Put your fingers slightly apart on the screen, and then pinch your fingers together to reduce the page; with your fingers already pinched together, place them on the screen, and then move them apart to enlarge the page.

9. Press the Home button to go back to the Home screen.

Display and Use the On-Screen Keyboard

1. iPad has a built-in keyboard that appears whenever you're in a text-entry location, such as a search field or e-mail message. Tap the Notes icon on the Home screen to open this easy-to-use notepad.

2. Tap the note; the on-screen keyboard appears.

3. Type a few words using the keyboard. To get the widest keyboard display possible, rotate your iPad to be in land-scape orientation (horizontal) (see **Figure 2-6**).

Tap in the note

then use keyboard to enter text

Figure 2-6

4. If you make a mistake (and you will when you first use it), use the backspace key (the key in the top-right corner with a little "x" on it) to delete text to the left of the insertion point.

5. To move to a new paragraph, press the Return button, just as you would on a regular computer keyboard.

6. To type numbers and some symbols, press one of the number keys (labeled .?123) located on either side of the spacebar (refer to **Figure 2-6**). Characters on the keyboard change. If you type a number and then tap the spacebar, the keyboard automatically returns to the letter keyboard. To return to the letter keyboard at any time, simply tap one of the letter keys on either side of the spacebar (labeled ABC).

7. Use the Shift buttons just as you would on a regular keyboard to type uppercase letters or alternate characters.

8. Double-tap the Shift key to turn the Caps Lock feature on; tap the Shift key again to turn it off. (You can control whether this features is available in iPad Settings).

9. To type a variation on a symbol (for example, to get alternate currency symbols when you press the dollar sign on the number keyboard), press the key and drag slightly; a set of alternate symbols appears (see **Figure 2-7**). Note that this works only on some symbols.

10. To hide the keyboard, press the Keyboard key in the bottom-right corner.

11. Tap the Home button to close Notes.

 To type a period and space, just double-tap the spacebar.

To type a number and automatically be returned to the alpha keys, press a .?123 key and slide your finger to the number you want to enter. When you release the key, you're back to the alpha keyboard.

A set of alternate symbols

Figure 2-7

Flick to Search

1. A search feature in iPad helps you find photos, music, e-mails, contacts, movies, and more. Press and drag from left to right on the Home screen to display the Spotlight screen. (You can also, from the primary Home screen, left-click the Home button to move one screen to the left.)

2. Tap in the Search iPad field; the keyboard appears (see **Figure** 2-8).

Tap here...

then enter a
search term

Figure 2-8

3. Begin entering a search term. In the example in **Figure** 2-9, I typed the letter "S" and came up with a contact, a couple of built-in apps, and some music I had downloaded, as well as a few e-mail messages. As you continue to type a search term, the results are narrowed down to match.

Figure 2-9

4. Tap an item in the search results to open it.

Explore the Status Bar

Across the top of your iPad screen is a Status bar (see **Figure** 2-10). Little icons in this area can provide some useful information, such as the time, your battery charge, or the status of your wireless connection. **Table** 2-1 lists some of the most common items you'll find in the Status bar:

iPad	3:30 PM	79%

Figure 2-10

Table 2-1		Common Status Bar Icons
Icon	**Item**	**What It Indicates**
	Wi-Fi	You're connected to a Wi-Fi network
	Activity	Something's in progress, such as a Web page loading
3:30 PM	Time	You guessed it: the time
	Screen Rotation Lock	The screen is locked and will not rotate when you turn the iPad
	Play	Media is playing
79%	Battery Life	The percentage of charge your battery has left (changes to a lightning bolt when battery is charging)

 If you have GPS, 3G, Bluetooth devices, or a connection to a virtual private network, symbols appear on the Status bar when these are active. The 3G icon will appear only with 3G-enabled iPad models. (If you can't even conceive of what a virtual private network is, my advice is, don't worry about this one.)

Take Inventory of Built-in Applications

iPad comes with certain functionality and applications (called *apps* for short) built in. When you look at your Home screen, you'll see icons for each of these. Here's an overview of what each one does (you'll find out more about every one of them as you move through the chapters in this book). Starting with the icons in the Dock (for more on the Dock, see the "Meet the Multi-Touch Screen" task, earlier in this chapter) and going from left to right are:

➡ **Safari:** A Web browser, similar to Internet Explorer, which you may have used on a Windows computer. You use Safari (see **Figure 2-11**) to navigate around the Internet, create and save bookmarks of favorite sites, and add Web clips to your Home screen so you can quickly visit favorite sites from there.

➡ **Mail:** The application you use to access mail accounts you have set up in iPad. Your e-mail will display without having to browse to the site or sign in. Then you can use tools to move among a few pre-set mail folders, read and reply to mail, and down-load attached photos to iPad. Read more about e-mail accounts in Chapter 6.

➡ **Photos:** This is the photo application in iPad (see **Figure 2-12**) that allows you to organize pictures in folders, e-mail photos to others, use a photo as your iPad wallpaper, or upload someone's picture to a contact record. You can also run slideshows of your photos. You can open albums, pinch or unpinch to shrink or expand photos, and scroll through photos with a swipe.

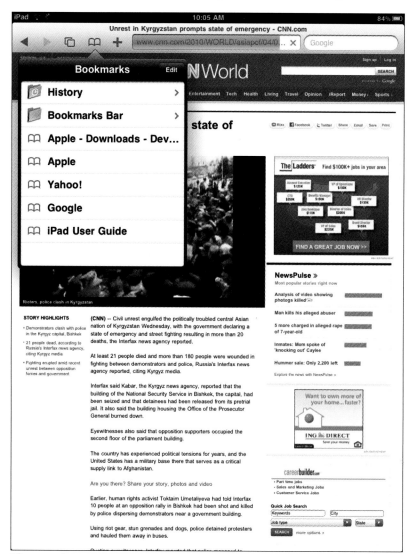

Figure 2-11

⟶ **iPod:** iPod is your media player. Use it to play movies, music, podcasts, audiobooks, or TV shows that
you've downloaded or transferred from your computer to the iPad.

Figure 2-12

Apps with icons above the Dock and closer to the top of the Home screen include:

 Calendar: Provides a handy on-screen daybook you can use to set up appointments and send alerts to remind you about them.

 Contacts: An address book feature (see **Figure 2-13**) where you can enter contact information (including photos, if you like, from your Photos app), and share contact information via e-mail. You can also use a search feature to find contacts easily.

 Notes: A simple notepad app where you can enter text or cut and paste text from a Web site. You can't do much except save your notes or e-mail them — there are no features for formatting text or inserting objects. But for simple notes on-the-fly, it's useful.

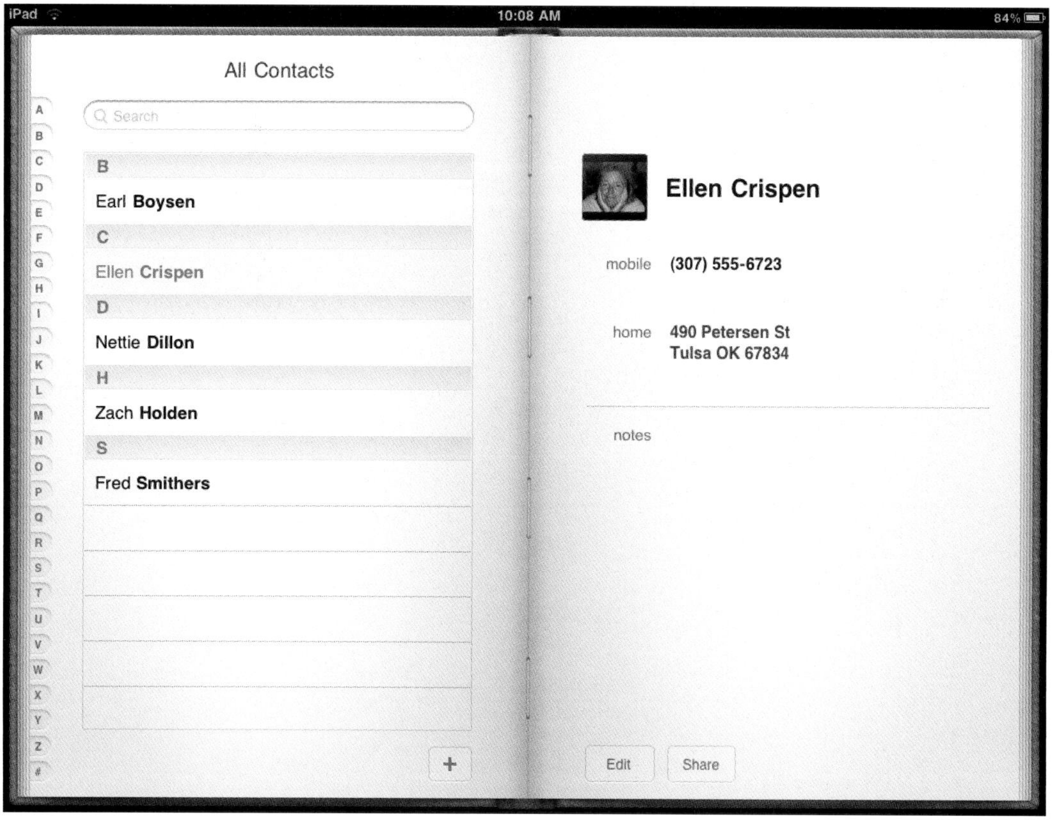

Figure 2-13

➠ **Maps:** This is a very cool iPad version of Google Earth. You can view classic maps (see **Figure 2-14**) or aerial views of addresses, get directions from one place to another by car, foot, or public transportation, and even view an address as if you were standing in front of the building at street level.

➠ **Videos:** A media player like iPod, but it specializes in playing videos and offers a few more features, such as chapter breakdowns and information about movie plots and cast.

Figure 2-14

⟶ **YouTube:** Tap it and you're taken to this popular online video-sharing site (see **Figure 2-15**) where you can watch videos people have posted, comment on them, share them with others, and so on.

⟶ **iTunes:** This takes you to the iTunes store where you can shop till you drop (or your iPad battery runs out of juice) for music, movies, TV shows, audiobooks, and podcasts and download them directly to your iPad. See Chapter 7 for more about how this works.

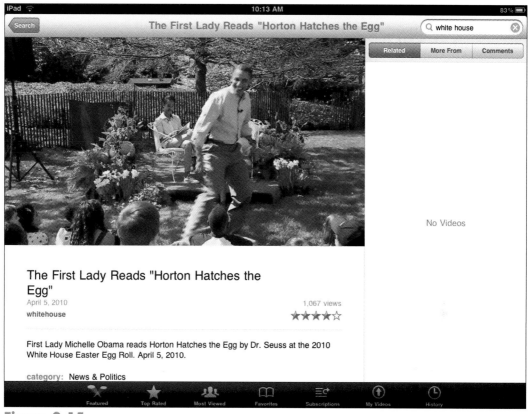

Figure 2-15

⟶ **App Store:** Tapping this icon takes you directly to an Apple online store where you can buy and download applications that do everything from enabling you to play games to building business presentations.

⟶ **Settings:** This isn't exactly an app, but it's an icon you should know about: It's the central location in iPad where you can make settings for various functions and do administrative tasks like setting up e-mail accounts or a password.

 iBooks is an eReader application that isn't built in to iPad out-of-the-box. It's free, but you'll have to download it from the App Store. Because iPad has been touted as a great *eReader* (a device that enables you to read books like Amazon's Kindle does), you should definitely consider getting it as soon as possible. For more about downloading applications for your iPad, see Chapter 8, and to work with the iBooks' eReader application itself, go to Chapter 9.

Put iPad to Sleep, Turn It Off, or Wake It Up

You've seen how simple it is to turn the power on for your iPad earlier in this chapter. Now it's time to put it to *sleep* (a state in which the screen goes black, but iPad can be quickly woken up again) or turn the power off to give the darn thing a rest. Here are the procedures you can use:

⟹ Press the Sleep/Wake button. iPad goes to sleep, the screen goes black, and it's locked.

⟹ Press the Home button or slide the Sleep/Wake slider. This wakes up iPad. Swipe the on-screen arrow on the Slide to Unlock bar (see **Figure 2-16**) to unlock the iPad.

⟹ Press and hold the Sleep/Wake button until the Slide to Power Off bar appears at the top of the screen, and then swipe the bar. You've just turned off your iPad.

 iPad automatically goes into sleep mode after a few minutes of inactivity. You can change the time interval at which it sleeps by adjusting the Auto-Lock feature in Settings. See this book's companion Cheat Sheet on the Web to review tables of various Settings.

Figure 2-16

Getting Going

*Y*our first step in getting to work with iPad is to make sure that the battery is charged. Next, if you want to buy or get free content for your iPad from Apple, from movies to music, e-books to audiobooks, look into opening an iTunes account.

After that, connect your iPad to your computer and sync them so that you can exchange content between them (for example, transferring your saved photos or music to iPad).

This chapter also introduces you to the iPad User Guide, which you access through the Safari browser on your iPad. This is essentially your iPad help system that provides advice and information about your magical new device.

Charge the Battery

1. My iPad showed up fully charged, and let's hope yours did, too. But all batteries run down eventually, so one of your first priorities is to know how to recharge your battery. Gather your iPad, connector cord, and power adapter.

2. Gently plug the USB connector (the smaller of the two connectors) on the end of the connector cord into the power adapter.

3. Plug the other end of the cord into the cord connector slot on the iPad (see **Figure 3-1**).

Attach the USB connector...to the power adapter.

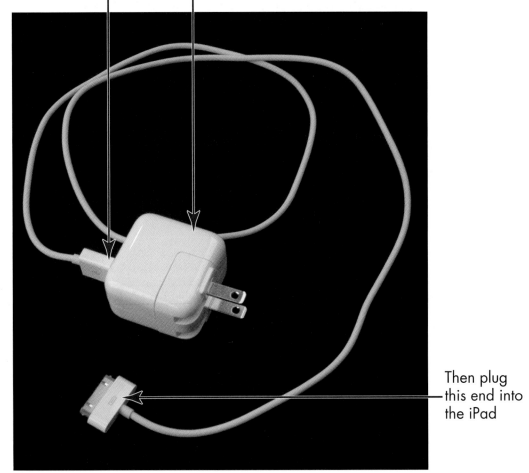

Then plug this end into the iPad

Figure 3-1

4. Unfold the two metal prongs on the power adapter (refer to **Figure 3-1**) so they extend from it at a 90-degree angle, and plug the adapter into a wall outlet.

If you buy the iPad Dock or the iPad Keyboard Dock accessory, you can charge your iPad while it's resting in the dock. Just plug the larger connector into the back of the dock instead of the bottom of the iPad.

Download iTunes to Your Computer

1. Download the iTunes application to your computer so you have the option of using it to *sync* (transfer) downloaded content to your iPad. Go to www.apple.com/itunes through your computer's browser.

2. Click the iTunes Free Download link shown in **Figure 3-2**. In the screen that follows, click the Download Now button.

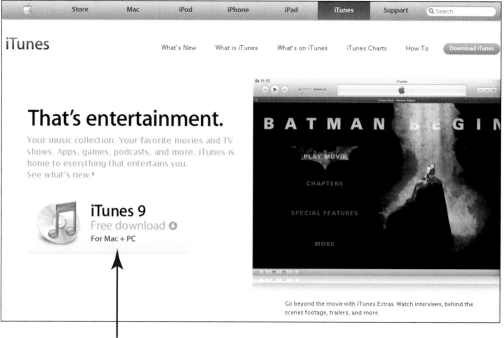

Click this link

Figure 3-2

3. In the dialog that appears (see **Figure 3-3**), click Run. The iTunes application downloads.

Click Run

Figure 3-3

4. When the download is complete, another dialog appears asking if you want to run the software. Click Run and the iTunes Installer appears (see **Figure 3-4**).

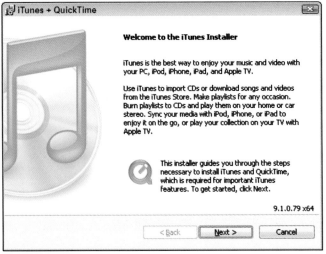

Figure 3-4

5. Click Next.

6. Click the I Accept the Terms of the License Agreement check box in the following dialog and click Next.

7. Review the installation options and click to deselect ones you don't want to use, and then click the Install button shown in **Figure 3-5**. A dialog appears, showing the installation progress.

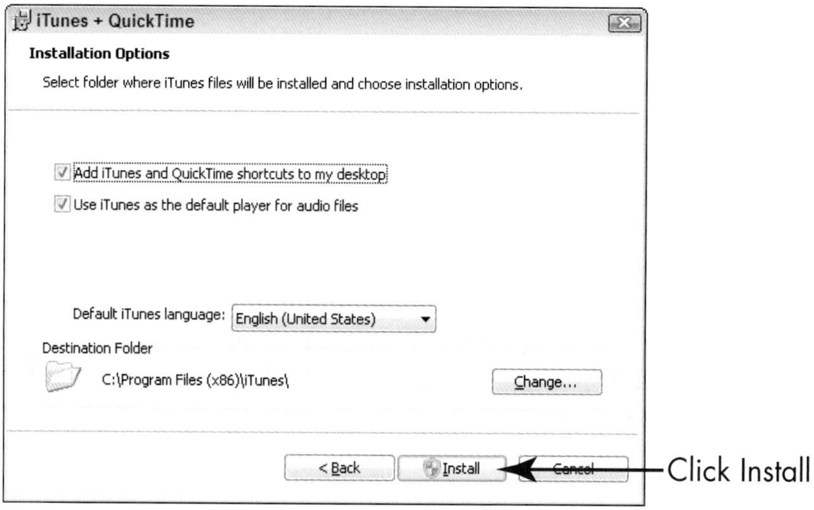

iTunes + QuickTime

Installation Options

Select folder where iTunes files will be installed and choose installation options.

☑ Add iTunes and QuickTime shortcuts to my desktop
☑ Use iTunes as the default player for audio files

Default iTunes language: English (United States) ▾

Destination Folder

C:\Program Files (x86)\iTunes\   Change...

< Back   Install   Cancel   ──Click Install

Figure 3-5

8. When a dialog appears telling you the installation is complete, click Finish. You'll have to restart your computer for the configuration settings made during the installation to take effect.

As of this writing, iTunes 9.1 is the latest version of this software. iTunes 9.1 requires that you have Windows XP or later on your PC, or Mac OS X version 10.4.11 or later on your Apple computer.

Get an iTunes Account for Music, Movies, and More

1. To be able to buy or download free items from the Apple Store on your iPad, you must open an iTunes account.

First, open iTunes (this is the application downloaded to your computer in the preceding task. You can open iTunes from your computer's Start menu in Windows or by clicking the iTunes item in the Mac Dock).

2. Choose the Store menu and select Create Account from the menu that appears (see **Figure 3-6**).

Select this option

Figure 3-6

3. In the Welcome to the iTunes Store screen that appears, click Continue.

4. In the following screen (see **Figure 3-7**), click to select the I Have Read and Agree to the iTunes Terms and Conditions check box, and click the Continue button.

5. In the Create iTunes Store Account (Apple ID) screen that follows (see **Figure 3-8**), fill in the information fields, click the last two check boxes to deselect them if you don't want to get e-mail from the Apple Store, and click the Continue button.

6. In the Provide a Payment Method screen that appears (see **Figure 3-9**), enter your payment information and then click the Continue button.

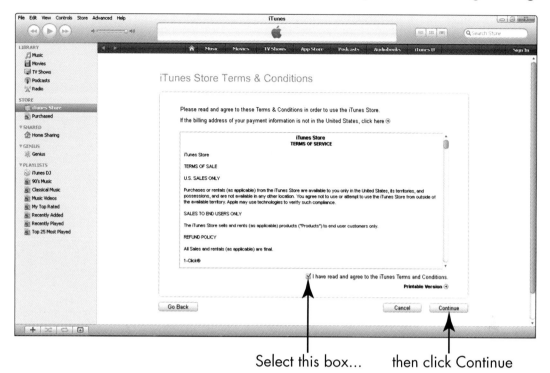

Select this box... then click Continue

Figure 3-7

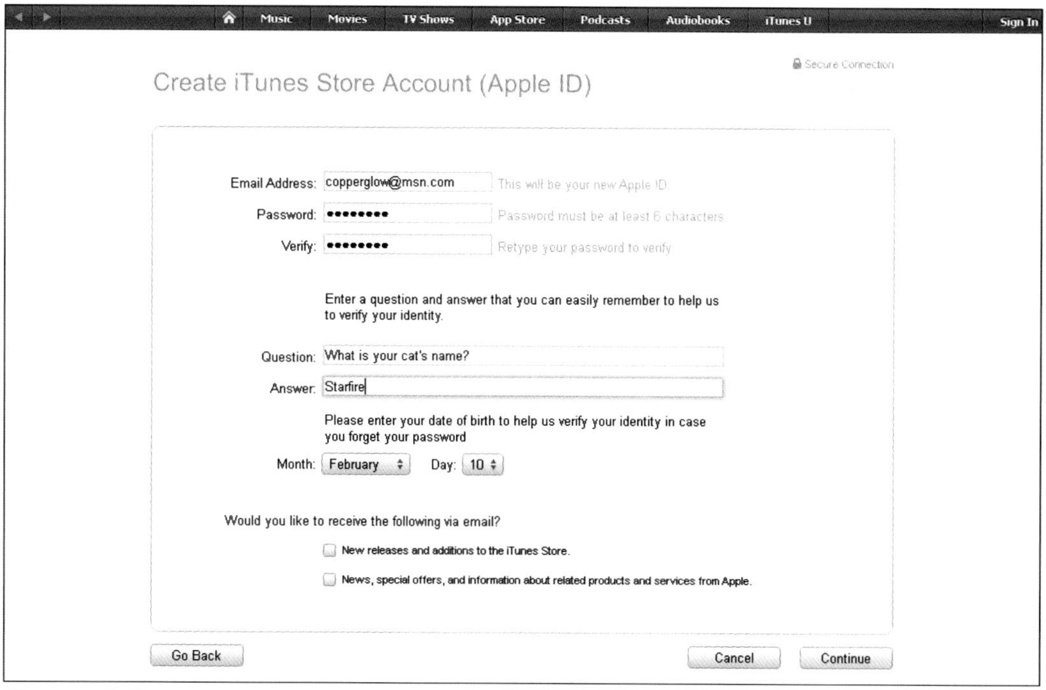

Figure 3-8

7. The screen shown in **Figure** 3-10 appears, confirming that your account has been opened. Click the Done button to return to the iTunes store.

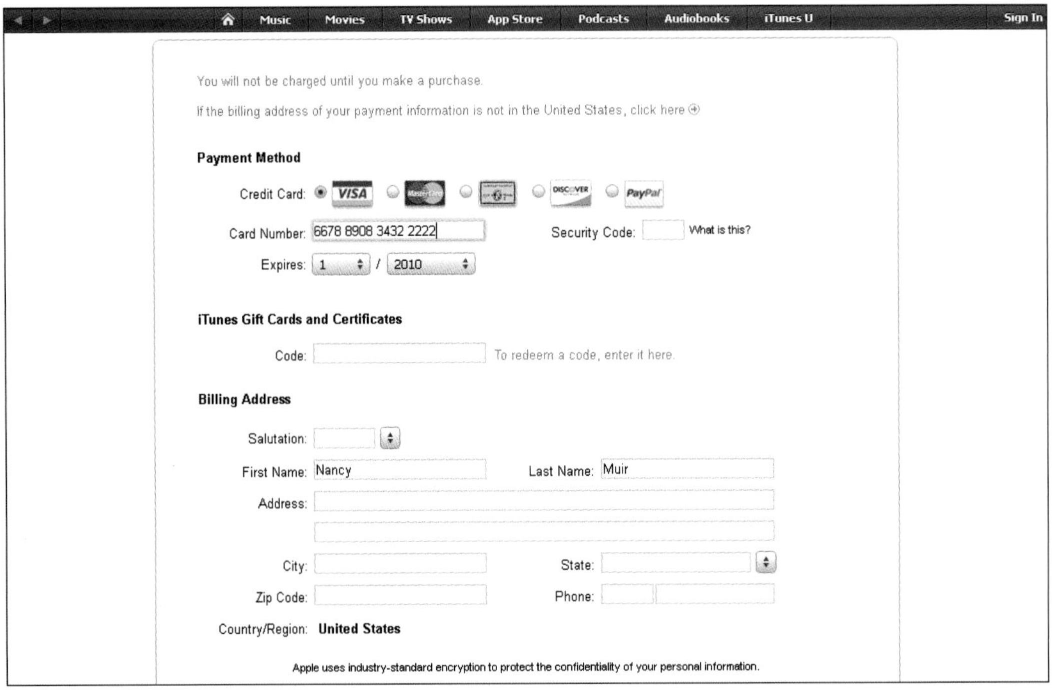

Figure 3-9

Make iPad Settings Using iTunes

1. Open your iTunes software (on a Windows computer, click Start⇨All Programs⇨iTunes; on a Mac, click the iTunes icon in the Dock).

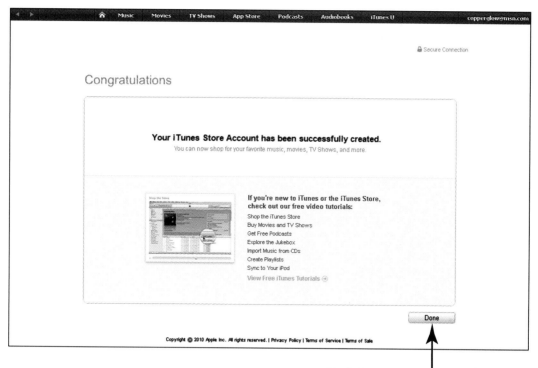

Click Done to return to the store

Figure 3-10

2. iTunes opens and your iPad is listed in the Devices section of the left pane, as shown in **Figure 3-11.** Click on your iPad and a series of tabs displays. These tabs offer information about your iPad and settings for items such as how to download music, movies, or podcasts (you can see the simple choices on the Music tab in **Figure 3-12**). The settings relate to what kind of content you want to download, and whether you want to download it automatically when you sync or do it manually. See **Table 3-1** for an overview of the settings that are available on each tab.

Click on your iPad... to display this series of tabs

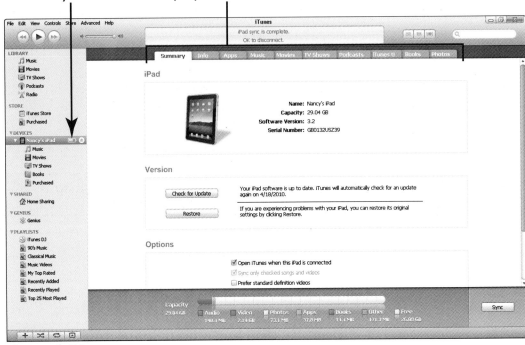

Figure 3-11

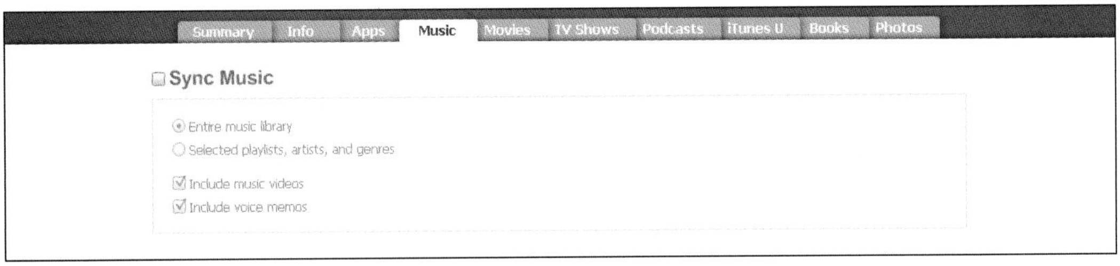

Figure 3-12

3. Make all settings for the types of content you plan to obtain on your computer and sync to your iPad, and then click the Sync button in the bottom right-hand corner to sync files with the iPad.

Table 3-1	iPad Settings in iTunes
Tab	**Description**
Summary	Perform updates to iPad software and set general sync options.
Info	Choose what information to sync: Contacts, Calendars, E-mail, Bookmarks, Notes.
Apps	Sync apps you've downloaded to your computer to iPad.
Music	Choose what music to download to your iPad when you sync.
Movies	Select the option to automatically download movies or not.
TV Shows	Choose which shows and episodes to automatically sync.
Podcasts	Choose which podcasts and episodes to automatically sync.
iTunes U	Select the course collections and items to sync to iPad.
Books	Choose to sync all or selected books to iPad.
Photos	Choose the folders from which you want to download photos.

Sync iPad to Your Computer

1. Now that you've made settings for what content to download in iTunes (see the preceding task), you must use the data connection cord to connect your iPad and computer to sync files, contacts, and calendar settings. With iTunes downloaded to your computer and an iTunes account set up, plug the data connection cord into your iPad (using the wider connector).

2. Plug the other end of the cord into a USB port on your computer.

3. iTunes opens and shows an item in the left pane for your iPad and an icon indicating that it's syncing (see **Figure 3-13**). Your iPad screen shows the words "Sync in Progress."

Icon indicating the iPad is syncing

Figure 3-13

4. When the syncing is complete, your Home screen returns on the iPad, and iTunes shows the message in **Figure 3-14** indicating that the iPad sync is complete and that it's okay for you disconnect the cable. Any media you chose to have transferred in your iTunes settings, and any new photos in the folder on your computer containing pictures, have been transferred to your iPad.

iTunes lets your know when syncing is complete

Figure 3-14

View the User Guide Online

1. The iPad User Guide is equivalent to the help system you may have used on a Windows or Mac computer. You access it online as a bookmarked site on the Safari browser. From the iPad Home screen, tap Safari.

2. Tap the Bookmark icon. In the Bookmarks menu that appears (see **Figure 3-15**), tap iPad User Guide.

Tap this option

Figure 3-15

3. Tap a topic on the left to display subtopics, as shown in **Figure 3-16**.

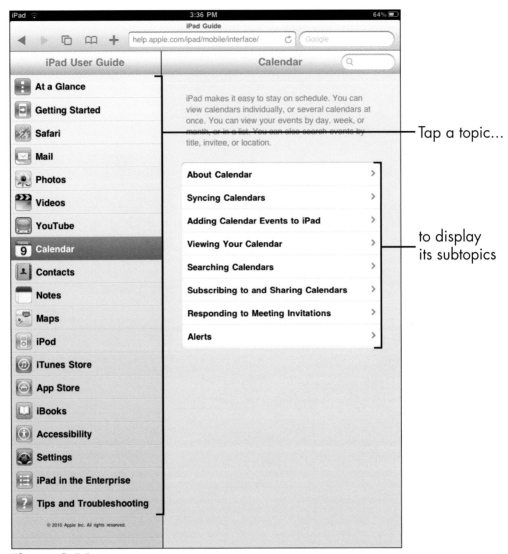

Figure 3-16

4. Tap a subtopic to display information about it, as shown in **Figure 3-17**.

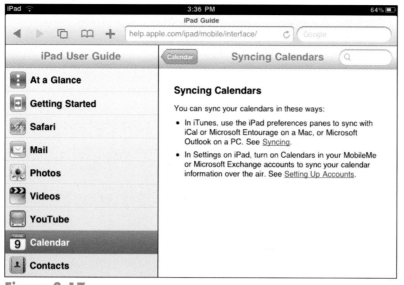

Figure 3-17

5. Tap any link in the subtopic information to access additional topics.

6. Tap the Home screen button to close the browser.

 You can also find a PDF version of the User Guide on your computer by going to this address: `http://manuals.info.apple.com/en_US/iPad_User_Guide.pdf`.

Accessibility and Ease of Use

*i*Pad users are all different, and some face visual or hearing challenges. If you're one of those folks, you'll be glad to hear that iPad offers some handy accessibility features.

To help you read your screen more easily, you can adjust the brightness or wallpaper. There's also a zoom feature that lets you enlarge the screen even more than the standard zoom feature does. There's even a black-and-white screen option which offers a black background with white lettering that some people find easier to read. You can also set up a feature called VoiceOver to read on-screen commands out loud.

If hearing is your challenge, you can do the obvious and adjust the system volume. There's also a setting for mono audio that's useful when you're wearing headphones. With this setting, instead of breaking up sounds in a stereo effect you get the entire sound in each ear. If you have more trouble hearing in one ear than the other, this option can help make sounds clearer. Finally, Speak Auto-text is a feature that iPad uses to tell you when any auto-corrections or capitalizations are made to text you enter in any iPad application.

Get ready to . . .

Set Brightness

1. Especially when using iPad as an eReader, you may find a little less bright screen reduces strain on your eyes. To begin, tap the Settings icon on the Home screen.

2. In the Settings dialog shown in **Figure 4-1,** tap Brightness & Wallpaper.

Tap this option...   then adjust the brightness

iPad	9:37 AM	81 %

Settings   **Brightness & Wallpaper**

Wi-Fi   2WIRE148

Brightness & Wallpaper

Picture Frame   Auto-Brightness   OFF

General

Mail, Contacts, Calendars   Wallpaper

Safari

iPod

Video

Photos

Store

Figure 4-1

3. To control brightness manually, tap the Auto-Brightness On/Off button (refer to **Figure 4-1**) to turn it off.

4. Tap and drag the Brightness slider to the right to make the screen brighter, or to the left to make it dimmer.

5. Tap the Home button to close the Settings dialog.

If glare from the screen is a problem for you, consider getting a screen protector. This thin film not only protects your screen from damage, but can also reduce glare.

Change the Wallpaper

1. The picture of a mountain lake that's the default iPad image may be pretty, but it's also pretty dark. Choosing different wallpaper may help you to see all the icons on your Home screen. Start by tapping the Settings icon on the Home screen.

2. In the Settings dialog, tap Brightness & Wallpaper.

3. In the Brightness & Wallpaper settings that appear, tap the arrow to the right of the Wallpaper section (see **Figure** 4-2).

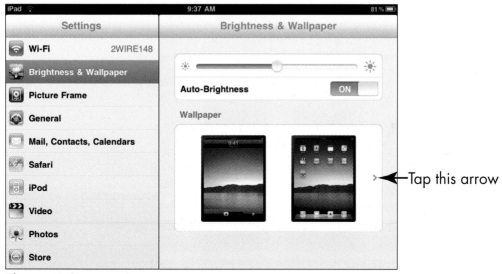

Figure 4-2

4. The options shown in **Figure** 4-3 appear. Tap Wallpaper and all built-in wallpaper images are displayed.

Tap this option

Figure 4-3

5. Tap on a wallpaper selection in the Wallpaper dialog (see **Figure** 4-4) to set it. A preview of it appears onscreen.

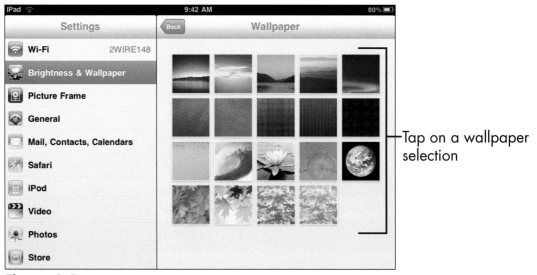

Tap on a wallpaper selection

Figure 4-4

6. Tap on the Set Home Screen button (see **Figure** 4-5). Alternatively, you can tap Set Lock Screen to use the image only when the screen is locked, or you can tap Set

Both to use the image for both the wallpaper and when the screen is locked.

———Tap this button

Figure 4-5

7. Tap the Home button and you return to your Home screen with the new wallpaper set as the background.

 You can also use your own picture for your wallpaper. In Step 4 above, instead of choosing Wallpaper tap Saved Photos to browse your saved photos, select the picture you want to assign, and then resume with Step 6 above to apply that screen to your iPad.

Turn on Zoom

1. The Zoom feature enlarges the contents displayed on the iPad screen when you double-tap the screen with three fingers. Tap the Settings icon on the Home screen and then tap General. In the General settings, tap Accessibility. The Accessibility dialog shown in **Figure** 4-6 appears.

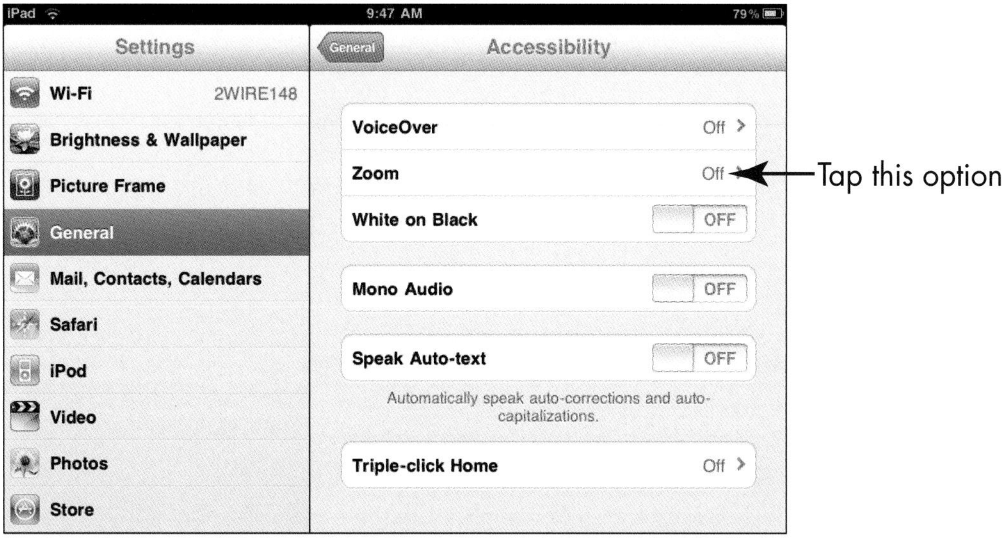

———Tap this option

Figure 4-6

2. Tap Zoom (refer to **Figure** 4-6).

3. In the Zoom dialog shown in **Figure** 4-7, tap the Zoom On/Off button to turn the feature on.

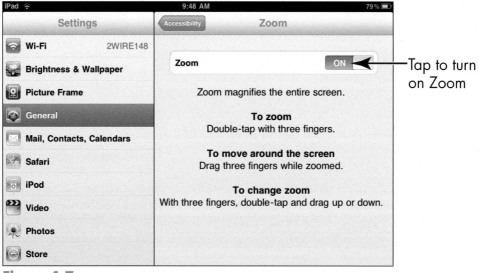

Figure 4-7

4. Now go to a Web site (www.wiley.com, for example) and double-tap the screen using three fingers; it enlarges (see **Figure** 4-8).

5. Press three fingers on the screen and drag to move around it.

6. Double-tap with three fingers again to go back to regular magnification.

7. Tap the Home screen to close Settings.

 This Zoom feature works pretty much everywhere in iPad: in Photos, on Web pages, in your Mail, in iPod and Video — give it a try!

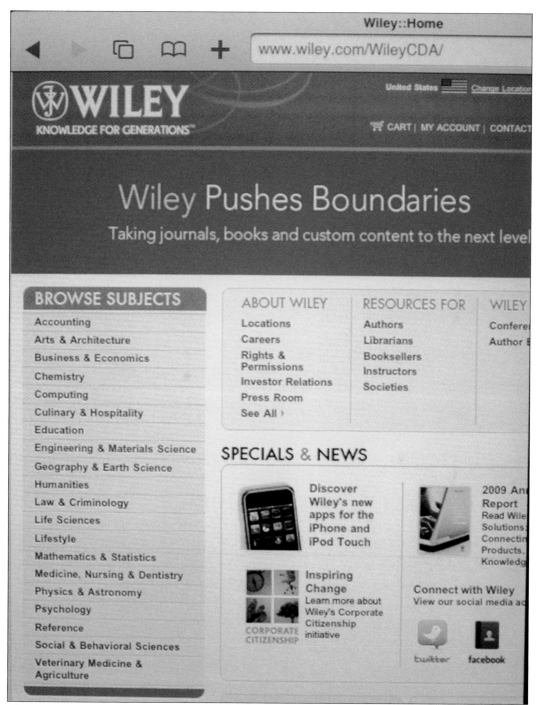

Figure 4-8

Turn on White on Black

1. White on Black is an accessibility setting that reverses colors on your screen so backgrounds are black and text is white. To turn this feature on, tap the Settings icon on the Home screen.

2. Tap General and then tap Accessibility.

3. In the Accessibility dialog shown in **Figure** 4-9, tap the White on Black On/Off button to turn it on.

iPad 🛜	9:47 AM	79% 🔋

Settings

⬅ General **Accessibility**

Wi-Fi	2WIRE148
Brightness & Wallpaper	
Picture Frame	
General	
Mail, Contacts, Calendars	
Safari	
iPod	
Video	
Photos	
Store	

VoiceOver	Off >
Zoom	Off >
White on Black	OFF

—Tap to turn on White on Black

| Mono Audio | OFF |

| Speak Auto-text | OFF |
Automatically speak auto-corrections and auto-capitalizations.

| Triple-click Home | Off > |

Figure 4-9

4. The colors on the screen reverse, as shown in **Figure** 4-10. Tap the Home button to leave the Settings.

 The White on Black feature works great in some places and not so well in others. For example, in the Photos application, pictures appear almost as photo negatives. Your Home screen image will likewise look a bit strange. And don't even think of playing a video with this feature turned on! However, if you need help reading text, it can be very useful in several applications.

Figure 4-10

Set Up VoiceOver

1. VoiceOver reads the names of screen elements and settings to you, but it also changes the way you provide input to iPad. In Notes, for example, you can have VoiceOver read the name of the Notes button to you, and when you enter Notes, read any words or characters you've entered, and tell you if features such as AutoCorrect are on. To turn the feature on, tap the Settings icon on the Home screen. Tap General and then tap Accessibility.

2. In the Accessibility dialog shown in **Figure 4-11**, tap the VoiceOver button.

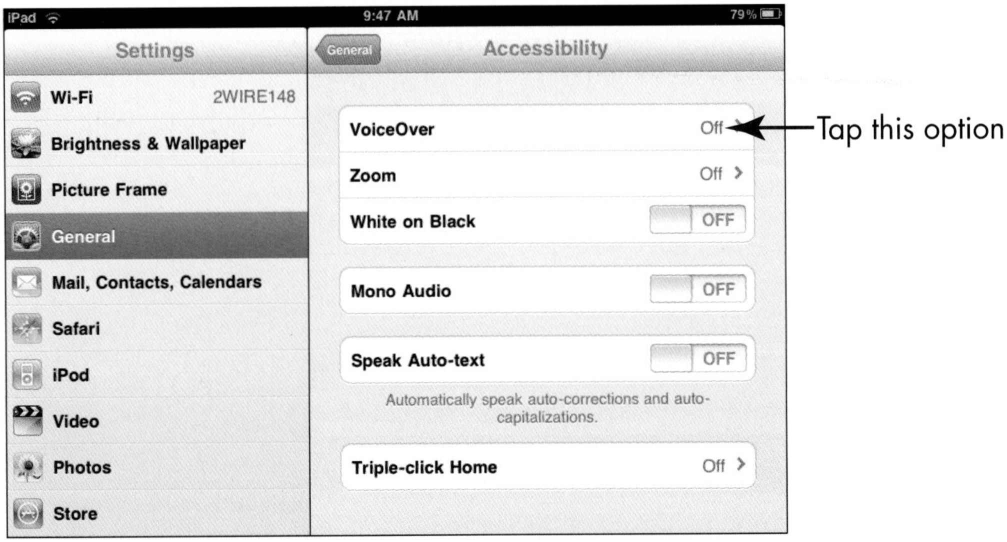

Tap this option

Figure 4-11

3. In the VoiceOver dialog shown in **Figure 4-12,** tap the VoiceOver On/Off button to turn it on. The first time you turn on the feature, you'll see a dialog noting that turning on VoiceOver changes gestures used to interact with iPad. Tap OK to proceed.

4. Tap the Practice VoiceOver Gestures button to select it, and then double-tap to open it (this is the new method of tapping that VoiceOver activates). It's important that you first single-tap to select an item such as a button, which causes VoiceOver to read the name of the button to you. Then double-tap the button to activate its function (VoiceOver reminds you to do this if you turn on Speak Hints, which is a help when you first use VoiceOver but gets annoying after a short time).

5. Tap the Speaking Rate field, and VoiceOver speaks the name of the item. Double-tap the slider; if you found the rate of the voice too slow or fast, move the slider to the left to slow it down or the right to speed it up.

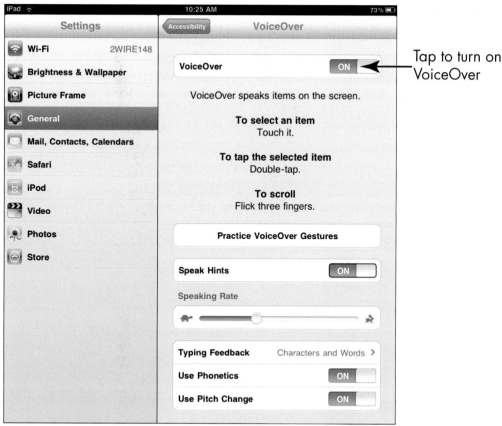

Tap to turn on VoiceOver

Figure 4-12

6. If you'd like VoiceOver to read words or characters to you (for example, in the Notes app), double-tap Typing Feedback.

7. In the Typing Feedback dialog, tap to select the option you prefer. Words will read words, but not characters such as "dollar sign." Characters and Words reads both.

8. Tap the Home button to return to the Home screen. Review the next task to find out how to navigate your iPad now that you have turned VoiceOver on.

You can change the language that VoiceOver speaks. In General settings, choose International, then Language, and select another language. This will, however, also change the language used for labels on Home icons and various settings and fields in iPad.

 You can use the Set Triple-Click Home setting to help you more quickly turn the VoiceOver and White on Black features on and off. In the Accessibility dialog, tap Triple-Click Home. In the dialog that appears, choose what you want a triple-click of the Home button to do: toggle VoiceOver on or off; toggle White on Black on or off; or display a menu of options using the Ask choice. Now a triple-click with a single finger on the Home button provides you with the options you selected wherever you go in iPad.

Use VoiceOver

Now that VoiceOver is turned on, you need to learn how to use it. I won't kid you; it's hard at first, but you'll get the hang of it! Here are the main on-screen gestures you should know:

➡ Tap an item to select it, and VoiceOver speaks its name.

➡ Now, double-tap the selected item to activate it.

➡ Flick three fingers to scroll.

Table 4-1 provides additional gestures that will help you use VoiceOver. I suggest that, if you want to use this feature often, you read the section of the iPad online User Guide, which goes into a great deal of detail about the ins and outs of using VoiceOver.

Table 4-1	VoiceOver Gestures
Gesture	**Effect**
Flick right or left	Select next or preceding item
Tap with two fingers	Stop speaking current item
Flick two-fingers up	Read everything from the top of the screen
Flick two-fingers down	Read everything from the current position
Flick up or down with three fingers	Scroll one page at a time
Flick right or left with three fingers	Go to next or preceding page
Tap three fingers	Speak the scroll status (for example, line 20 of 100)
Flick four fingers up or down	Go to first or last element on a page
Flick four fingers right or left	Go to next or preceding section (as on a Web page)

 If tapping with two or three fingers seems difficult for you, try tapping with one finger from one hand and one or two from the other. When double- or triple-tapping, perform these gestures as quickly as you can for them to work.

Adjust the Volume

1. Though individual applications such as iPod and Video have their own volume settings, you can set your iPad system volume as well to help you hear what's going on better. Tap the Settings icon on the Home screen.

2. In the General settings, tap Sounds.

3. In the Sounds dialog that appears (see **Figure** 4-13), tap and drag the slider to the right to increase the volume, or to the left to lower it.

Adjust iPad
volume here

Figure 4-13

4. Tap the Home button to close Settings.

 You can turn the sounds that iPad makes when certain events occur (such as receiving new mail or Calendar alerts) on or off in the Sounds dialog. These sounds are turned on by default. Conversely, if you need the audio clue and one of these has been turned off, just tap the On/Off button for an item to turn it back on.

Use Mono Audio

1. Stereo used in headphones breaks up sounds so that you hear a portion in one ear and a portion in the other to simulate the way we actually hear sounds. However, if you're hard of hearing or deaf in one ear, you're getting only a portion of a sound in your hearing ear, which can be difficult. To turn on Mono Audio, which plays all sounds in each ear, tap the Settings icon on the Home screen.

2. In the General settings, tap Accessibility.

3. In the Accessibility dialog shown in **Figure** 4-14, tap the Mono Audio On/Off button to turn it on.

iPad 🛜	10:28 AM	72% 🔋

| Settings | ‹ General | Accessibility |

Wi-Fi   2WIRE148

Brightness & Wallpaper

Picture Frame

General

Mail, Contacts, Calendars

Safari

iPod

Video

Photos

Store

VoiceOver   Off ›

Zoom   Off ›

White on Black   OFF

Mono Audio   ON ⬅   Tap to turn on Mono Audio

Speak Auto-text   OFF

Automatically speak auto-corrections and auto-capitalizations.

Triple-click Home   Off ›

Figure 4-14

4. Tap the Home button to close Settings.

 If you have hearing challenges, another good feature that iPad provides is support for closed-captioning. In the Video player, you can use a closed-captioning feature to provide onscreen text for dialog and actions in a movie as it plays. For more about playing videos, see Chapter 12.

Have iPad Speak Auto-Text

1. Speak Auto-text is a feature that speaks auto-corrections and auto-capitalizations (two features that you can turn on with Keyboard settings). When you enter text in an application such as Word or Mail and then make either type of change, Speak Auto-text lets you know. To turn Speak Auto-text on, tap the Settings icon on the Home screen.

2. Under the General settings, tap Accessibility.

3. In the Accessibility dialog shown in **Figure** 4-15, tap the Speak Auto-text On/Off button to turn the feature on.

iPad 🔆	10:28 AM	72% 🔋

Settings		‹ General Accessibility
🔆 **Wi-Fi**	2WIRE148	**VoiceOver** Off ›
🖼 **Brightness & Wallpaper**		**Zoom** Off ›
🖼 **Picture Frame**		**White on Black** OFF
⚙ **General**		
✉ **Mail, Contacts, Calendars**		**Mono Audio** OFF
🧭 **Safari**		**Speak Auto-text** ON ◀
🎵 **iPod**		Automatically speak auto-corrections and auto-capitalizations.
📹 **Video**		
🌸 **Photos**		**Triple-click Home** Off ›
🛒 **Store**		

Tap to turn on Speak Auto-Text

Figure 4-15

4. Tap the Home button to leave the Settings.

Why would you want iPad to tell you when an auto-correction has been made? If you have vision challenges and you know you typed "ain't" when writing dialog for a character in your novel, but iPad corrected it to "isn't," you would want to know, right? Similarly, if you typed the poet's name e.e. Cummings and auto-capitalization corrected it (incorrectly), you need to know immediately so you can change it back again!

Part II

Taking the Leap Online

The 5th Wave   By Rich Tennant

"Hold on Barbara. I'm pretty sure there's an app for this."

Browsing the Internet with Safari

Getting on the Internet with your iPad is easy using its Wi-Fi or 3G capabilities. Once you're online, the built-in browser, Safari, is your ticket to a wide world of information, entertainment, education, and more. Safari will be familiar to you if you've used a Mac device before, though the way you move around will be new to you with your touch-screen iPad. If you've never used Safari, this chapter takes you by the hand and shows you all its ins and outs.

In this chapter, you discover how to connect your iPad to the Internet and navigate among Web pages. Along the way, you learn how to place a bookmark for a favorite site or place a Web clip on your Home screen. You can also view your browsing history, save online images to your Photo Library, or e-mail a hotlink to a friend.

Get ready to . . .

Connect to the Internet

How you connect to the Internet depends on which iPad model you own:

➟ The Wi-Fi–only iPad connects to the Internet only via a Wi-Fi network. You can set up such a network in your own home using your computer and some equipment from your Internet provider. You can also connect through public Wi-Fi networks referred to as *hotspots*. You'll probably be surprised to discover how many hotspots your town or city has: Look for Internet cafes, coffee shops, hotels, libraries, transportation centers such as airports or bus stations, and so on. Many of these businesses display signs alerting you to their free Wi-Fi.

➟ If you own a Wi-Fi and 3G-enabled iPad, you can still use a Wi-Fi connection, but you can also use a paid data network through AT&T to connect from just about anywhere via a cellular network.

When you're in range of a hotspot, if access to several nearby networks is available you may see a message asking you to tap on one to select it. After you select one (or if only one network is available), you will see a message similar to the one shown in **Figure 5-1.** If it's required, enter a network password, and then tap the Join button.

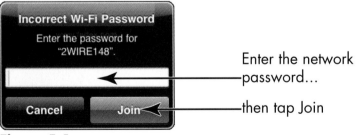

Figure 5-1

See Chapter 1 for more about the capabilities of different iPad models and the costs associated with 3G.

Free public Wi-Fi networks typically don't require a password. However, that means they're *unsecured*, so it's possible for someone else to track your online activities over the network. Avoid accessing financial accounts or sending sensitive e-mails when connected to a public hotspot.

Explore Safari

1. After you're connected to a network, tap the Safari button on the Home screen. Safari opens, probably displaying the Apple iPad home page the first time you go online with it (see **Figure 5-2**).

2. Double-tap the screen with a single finger to enlarge it, as shown in **Figure 5-3**. Double-tap again to return to the default screen size.

3. Put your finger on the screen and drag upward to scroll down on the page.

4. To return to the top of the Web page, put your finger on the screen and drag downward, or tap the Status bar at the top of the screen.

Bookmarks

Multiple Pages

Settings menu for Bookmarks,
Web Clips, and Mailing Links

Previous

Next

Address field   Status bar   Search field

Figure 5-2

Figure 5-3

 You can also use the pinch method to enlarge or reduce the size of a Web page on your screen. Using this method you can enlarge the screen to various sizes, giving you more flexibility than with the double-tap your finger method described in Step 2.

When you enlarge the screen, you get more control using two fingers to drag left to right or top to bottom on the page. In a reduced screen, one finger works fine for these gestures.

Navigate among Web Pages

1. Tap in the Address field. The on-screen keyboard appears, as shown in **Figure 5-4**.

2. Enter a Web address; for example, you can go to my Web site, www.techsmartsenior.com.

3. Tap the Go key on the keyboard (refer to **Figure 5-4**). The Web site appears.

- If, for some reason, a page doesn't display, tap the Reload icon on the right side of the address field.

- If Safari is loading a Web page and you change your mind, you can tap the Stop icon (the X) that appears on the right side of the address field during this process to stop loading the page.

4. Tap the Previous arrow to go backward to the first page.

5. Tap the Next arrow to go forward to the second page you displayed.

6. To follow a link to another Web page, tap the link with your finger. If you would like to view the destination Web address of the link before you tap it, just touch and hold the link and a menu appears that displays the address at the top, as shown in **Figure 5-5**.

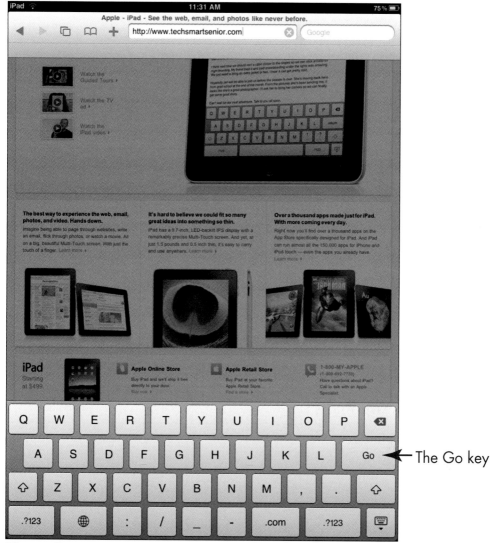

The Go key

Figure 5-4

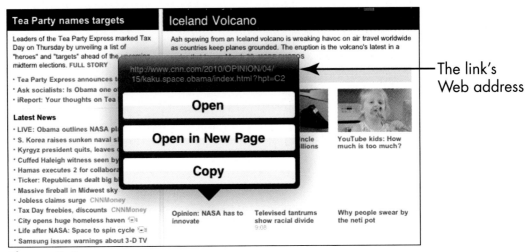

The link's
Web address

Figure 5-5

 By default, AutoFill is turned on in iPad, causing entries you make in fields such as the address field to automatically display possible matching entries. You can turn AutoFill off using iPad Settings.

View Browsing History

 1. As you move around the Web, your browser keeps a record of your browsing history. This can be handy when you visit a site that you want to view again but you forget its address. With Safari open, tap the Bookmark icon.

2. In the menu shown in **Figure 5-6,** tap History.

3. In the History list that appears (see **Figure 5-7**), tap a site to navigate to it.

 To clear the history, tap the Clear History button (refer to **Figure 5-7**). This is useful when you don't want your spouse or grandchildren seeing where you've been browsing for birthday or holiday presents!

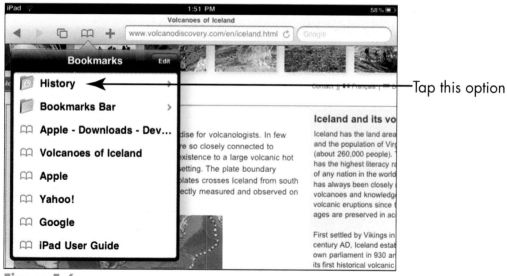

Tap this option

Figure 5-6

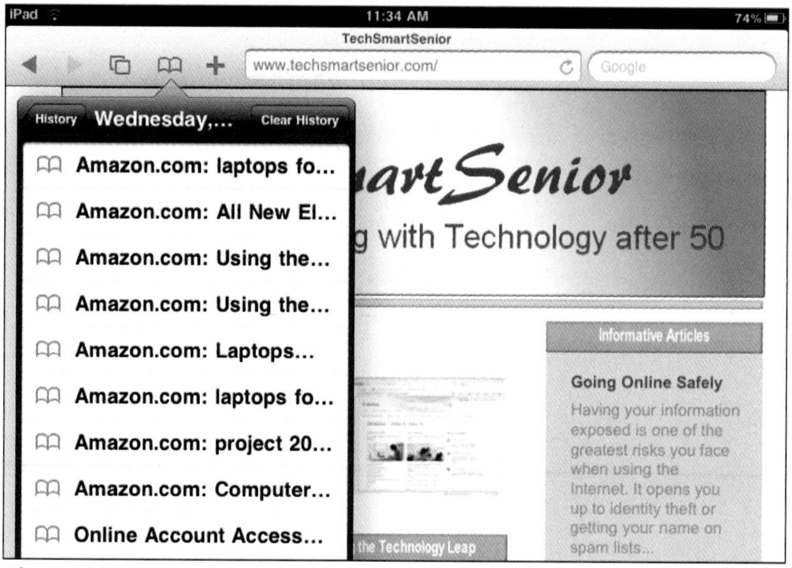

Figure 5-7

Display Web Pages as Thumbnails

1. Another great way to see Web sites you've visited recently is to display multiple pages as thumbnails on a single page. With Safari open, tap the Multiple Pages icon in the

Status bar. Recently visited pages are displayed as thumbnails, as shown in **Figure 5-8.**

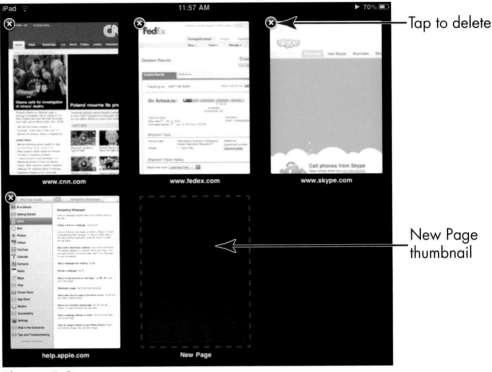

Figure 5-8

2. In this view, you can do several things:

- To delete a page from this view, tap the Delete icon in a Web site's upper-left corner (the circle with an X in it).

- To go to a new page, tap the New Page thumbnail and then tap in the Address field and enter a Web address.

- To go to a full view of any of the pages shown, tap it or pinch to enlarge it.

The Multiple Pages view has nine possible site slots. Clearing your history won't clear the multiple pages view of sites you visited recently. To remove sites from this view, you have to delete them one by one, or wait for them to be replaced by more recently visited sites.

Search the Web

1. If you don't know the address of the site you want to visit (or you want to do research on a topic or find something you need online), you need to get acquainted with Safari's search feature on iPad. By default, Safari uses the Google search engine. With Safari open, tap in the Search field (it's to the right of the Address field; refer to **Figure 5-2**). The on-screen keyboard appears (see **Figure 5-9**).

2. Enter a search word or phrase, and tap the Search key on your keyboard.

3. In the search results that are displayed, tap on a link to a site to visit it.

 You can change your default search engine from Google to Yahoo! In iPad Settings, tap Safari, and then tap Search Engine. Tap on Yahoo! and your default browser changes to Yahoo!.

 You can browse for specific items such as images, videos, or maps by tapping any of the links at the top of the Google screen. Also, tap the Advanced Search link to the right of Google's Search button to specify more search details and narrow your search.

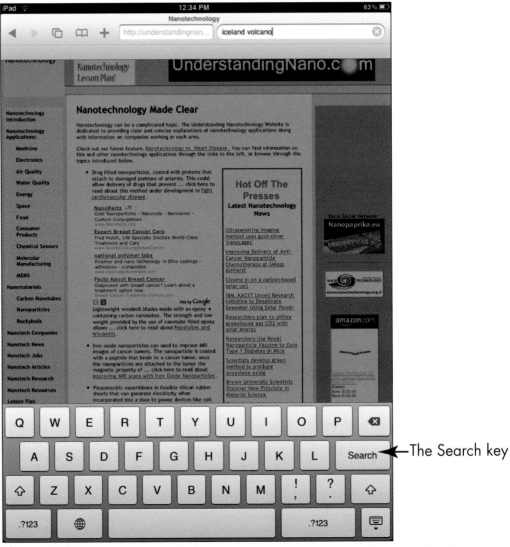

The Search key

Figure 5-9

Add and Use Bookmarks

1. Bookmarks are a way to save favorite sites so you can easily visit them again. With a site you want to bookmark displayed, tap the Add icon.

2. In the menu that appears (see **Figure 5-10**), tap Add
Bookmark.

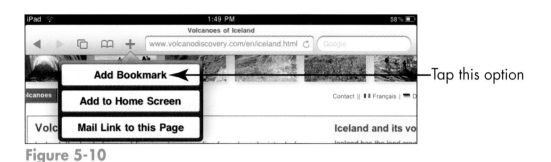

—Tap this option

Figure 5-10

3. In the Add Bookmark dialog shown in **Figure 5-11,** edit
the name of the bookmark, if you wish. To do so, tap the
name of the site and use the on-screen keyboard to edit
its name.

Edit the
name here

Figure 5-11

4. Tap the Save button.

 5. To go to the bookmark, tap the Bookmarks icon.

6. In the menu that appears (see **Figure 5-12**), tap the
bookmarked site you want to visit.

Tap a bookmarked site to visit it

Figure 5-12

 If you want to sync your bookmarks on your iPad browser to your computer or using your MobileMe account, connect your iPad to your computer and make sure the setting on the Info tab of iTunes has Sync Safari Bookmarks activated.

 When you tap the Bookmarks button, you can use the Bookmarks Bar option to create folders to organize your bookmarks. When you next add a bookmark you can then choose any folder to add the new bookmark to from the dialog that appears.

Add Web Clips to the Home Screen

1. Web Clips is a feature that allows you to save a Web site as an icon on your Home screen so you can go to it at any time with one tap. With Safari open and the site you want to add displayed, tap the Add icon.

2. In the menu that appears (see **Figure 5-13**), tap Add to Home Screen.

Figure 5-13

Tap this option

3. In the Add to Home dialog that appears (see **Figure 5-14**), you can edit the name of the site to be more descriptive, if you like. To do so, tap the name of the site and use the on-screen keyboard to edit its name.

Figure 5-14

Edit the name here

4. Tap the Add button. The site is added to your Home screen.

Remember that you can have up to 11 Home screens on your iPad, so all the Web Clips and apps you download have room to grow. If you want to delete an item from your Home screen for any reason, press and hold the icon on the Home screen until all the items on the screen start to jiggle and Delete icons appear on every item except pre-installed apps. Tap the Delete icon on the item you want to delete and it's gone. (To get rid of the jiggle, tap the Home button.)

Save an Image to Your Photo Library

1. Display a Web page that contains an image you want to copy.

2. Press and hold the image. The menu in **Figure 5-15** appears.

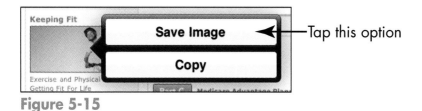

Figure 5-15

3. Tap Save Image. The image is saved to your library.

 Be careful about copying images from the Internet and using them for business or promotional activities. Most images are copyrighted in some fashion, and you may be violating that copyright if you use an image in a brochure for your association or a flyer for your community group. Note that some search engines, through their advanced search settings, offer the option of browsing only for images that aren't copyrighted.

Mail a Link

1. If you find a great site that you want to share, you can do so easily by sending a link in an e-mail. With Safari open and the site you want to share displayed, tap the Add icon.

2. In the menu shown in **Figure 5-16,** tap Mail Link to this Page.

Figure 5-16

3. In the message form that appears (see **Figure 5-17**), enter a recipient's e-mail address, subject, and your message.

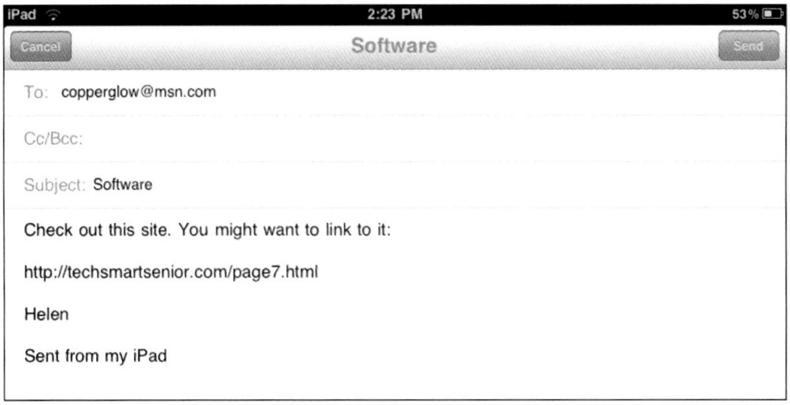

Figure 5-17

4. Tap Send, and the e-mail goes on its way.

 The e-mail will be sent from the e-mail account you have set up on iPad. For more about setting up an e-mail account, see Chapter 6.

Working with E-Mail in Mail

Staying in touch with others through an e-mail account is a great way to use your iPad. You can access an existing account using the handy Mail app supplied with your iPad, or, if the mail service has a Web-based interface, you can sign in using the Safari browser. Using Mail involves adding an e-mail account. Then you can use Mail to write, retrieve, and forward messages.

Mail offers a small set of folders for organizing your messages and a handy search feature. In this chapter, you learn all about Mail and its various features.

Get ready to . . .

Add a Gmail, Yahoo!, or AOL Account

1. You can add one or more e-mail accounts using iPad Settings. If you have a Gmail, Yahoo!, or AOL account, iPad pretty much automates the setup. To set up iPad to retrieve message from an e-mail account that you have with one of these three popular providers, first tap the Settings icon on the Home screen.

2. In the Settings dialog, tap Mail, Contacts, Calendars. The settings shown in **Figure 6-1** appear.

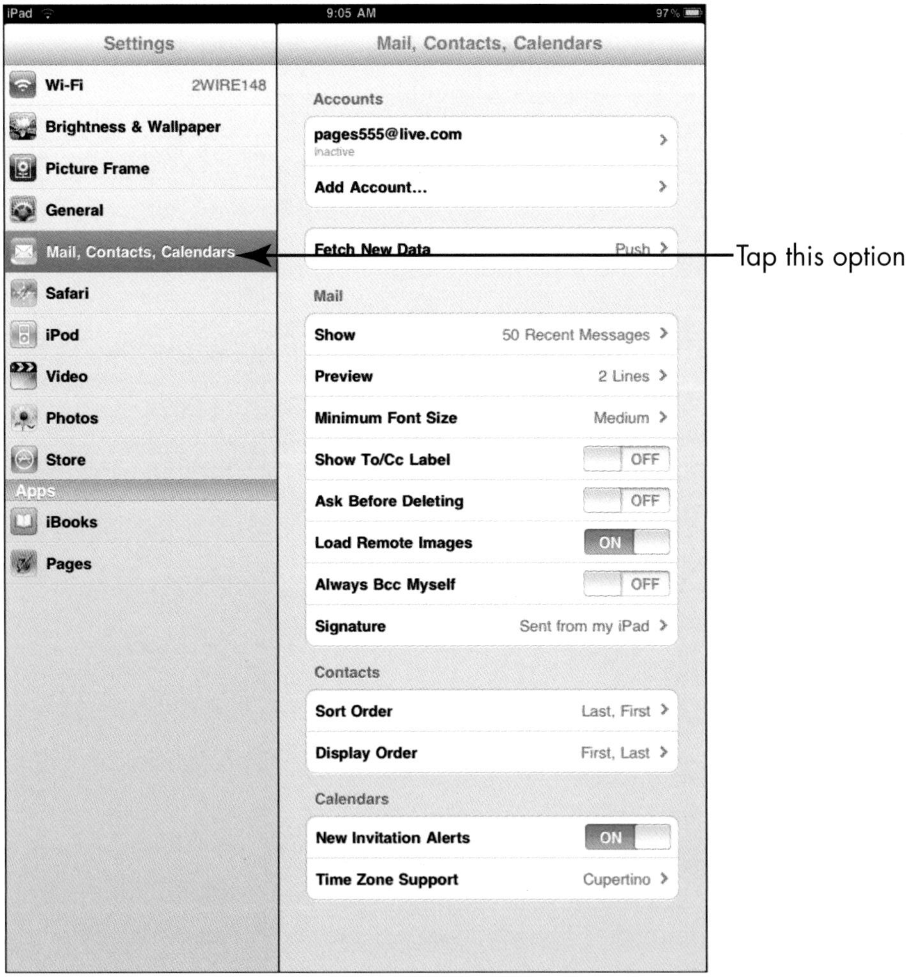

Tap this option

Figure 6-1

3. Tap Add Account. The options shown in **Figure 6-2** appear.

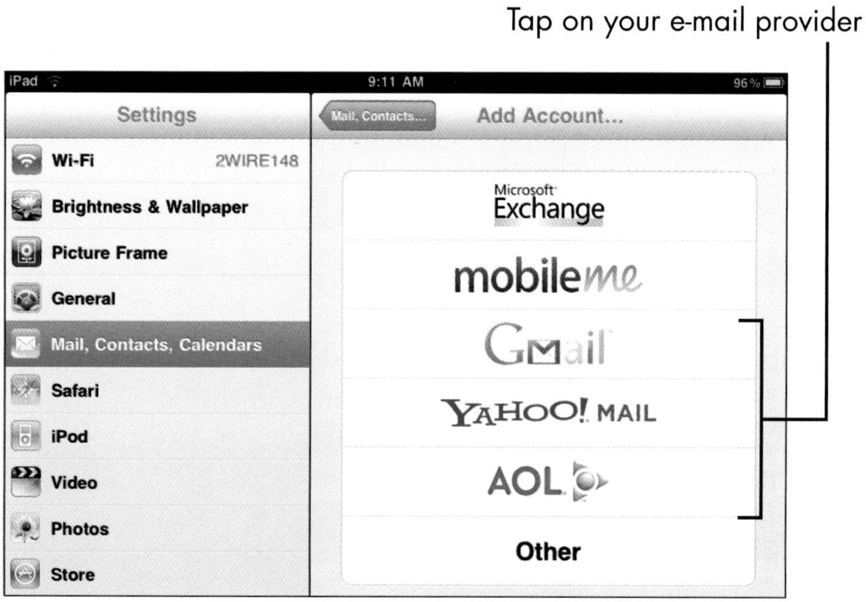

Tap on your e-mail provider

Figure 6-2

4. Tap Gmail, Yahoo! Mail, or AOL. Enter your account information in the form that appears (see **Figure 6-3**).

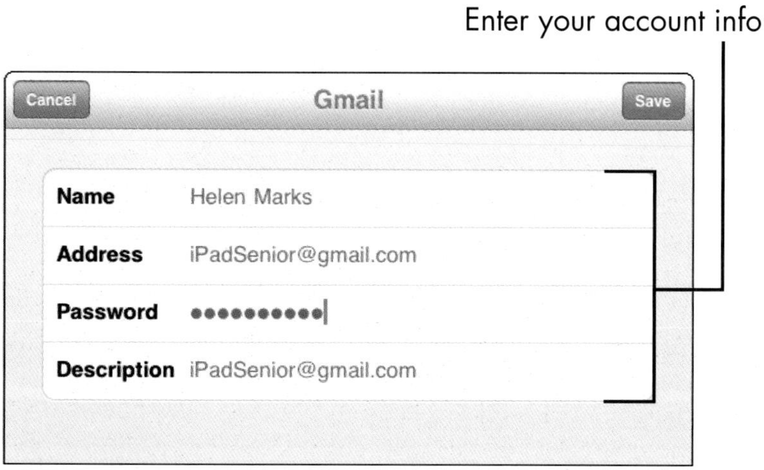

Enter your account info

Figure 6-3

5. After iPad takes a moment to verify your account information, tap Save. The account is saved and you can now
open it using Mail.

 If you have a Microsoft Exchange or Mobile Me
account, you can sync to your computer to exchange
contact and calendar information as well as e-mail.
See the iPad User Guide for more about these
options.

Set Up a POP3 E-Mail Account

1. You can also set up most popular e-mail accounts such as
Windows Live by obtaining the host name from the provider. To set up an existing account for an account with a
provider other than Gmail, Yahoo! or AOL, you need to
enter the account settings yourself. First, tap the Settings
icon on the Home screen.

2. In Settings, tap Mail, Contacts, Calendars, and then tap
Add Account.

3. In the screen that appears (refer to **Figure 6-2**), tap
Other.

4. The form in **Figure 6-4** appears. Enter your name, the
account Address, the Host Name (POP3 or IMAP, which
you can get from your provider), and your password.
iPad will probably add the Outgoing Mail Server information for you, but if it doesn't, tap SMTP and enter this
information.

5. Make sure the Account field is set to On, and then tap
Done to save the account, which you can now access
through Mail.

Cancel	pages555@live.com	Done

Account   **ON**

POP Account Information

Name	Nancy Muir
Address	pages123@live.com|
Description	pages123@live.com

Incoming Mail Server

Host Name	pop3.live.com
User Name	page7@live.com
Password	●●●●●●

Outgoing Mail Server

SMTP	smtp.live.com >

Advanced	>

Figure 6-4

 POP3 and *IMAP* are e-mail protocols (standards) that are used by many e-mail providers. By entering the POP3 or IMAP ingoing and outgoing (SMTP) server information, you can set up just about any e-mail provider's account in iPad.

 You can turn any e-mail account on or off by opening it in Settings and tapping the On/Off button.

Open Mail and Read Messages

1. Tap the Mail app icon located in the Dock on the Home screen (see **Figure 6-5**), which displays the number of unread e-mails in your Inbox in a red circle.

Tap this icon

Figure 6-5

2. In the Mail app, if you're holding the iPad in portrait orientation, tap the Inbox button to display the Inbox if the
Inbox contents aren't already displayed (see **Figure 6-6**).
If a list of mailboxes displays, tap the Inbox button. Note
that in landscape orientation, the Mailboxes/Inbox panel
is always displayed, but in portrait orientation you display it by clicking the Inbox button.

Tap this button...

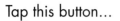

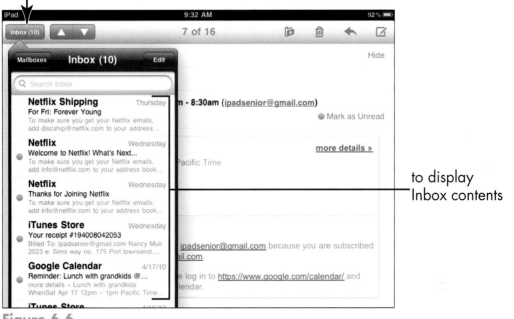

Figure 6-6

3. Tap a message to read it. It opens (see **Figure 6-7**).

4. If you need to scroll to see the entire message, just place your finger on the screen and flick upward to scroll down.

 You can tap the Hide button to hide the address details (the To field) so more of the message appears on your screen. To reveal the field again, tap the Details button (which becomes the Hide button when details are displayed).

 E-mail messages you haven't read are marked with a blue circle in your Inbox. After you read a message, the blue circle disappears. If you'd like, you can mark a read message as unread. This can help remind you to read it again later. With a message open, tap the Mark as Unread link on the right side.

Figure 6-7

 Some popular e-mail services *push* your e-mail to you. This means that a small indicator on the Mail icon on your Home screen indicates when you have new mail without you having to connect and retrieve mail. If you'd like to escape your e-mail now and then (or avoid having messages retrieved while at a public Wi-Fi hotspot), however, you can turn off this feature using the Fetch New Data feature of the Mail in Settings.

Reply to or Forward E-Mail

1. With an e-mail message open (see the previous task), tap the Reply/Forward button shown in **Figure 6-8**.

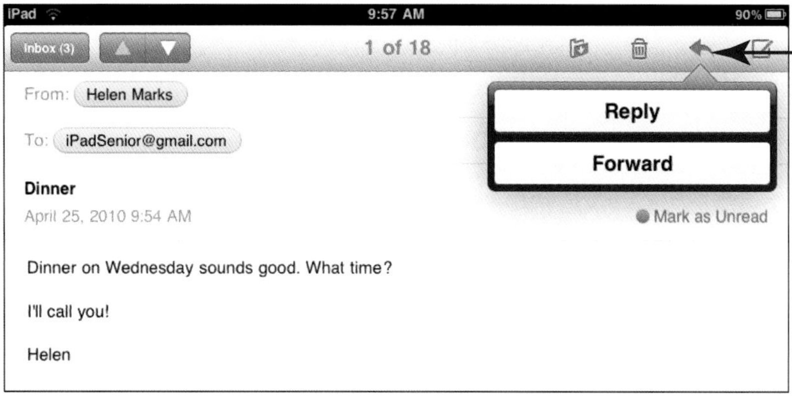

Tap the Reply/Foward button

Figure 6-8

2. Take one of the following actions:

- Tap Reply to respond to the sender of the message. The reply message form shown in **Figure 6-9** appears. Tap in the message body and enter a message.

- Tap Forward to send the message to somebody else. The form in **Figure 6-10** appears. Enter a recipient in the To field, then tap in the message body and enter a message.

Tap here to enter a reply

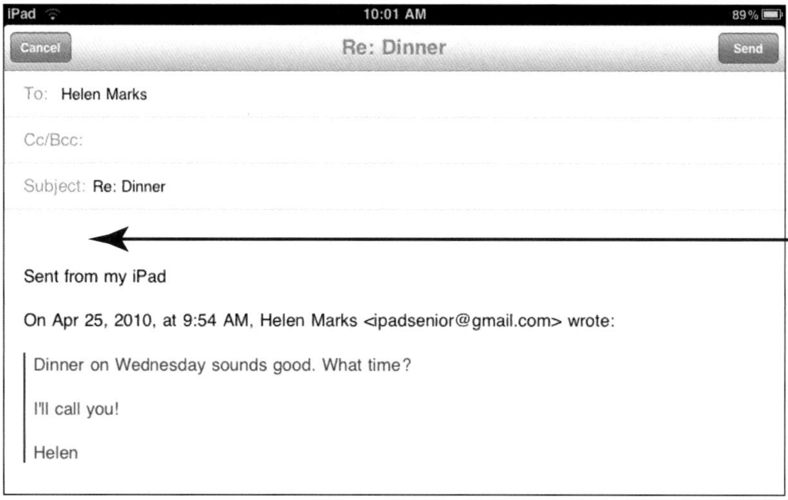

Figure 6-9

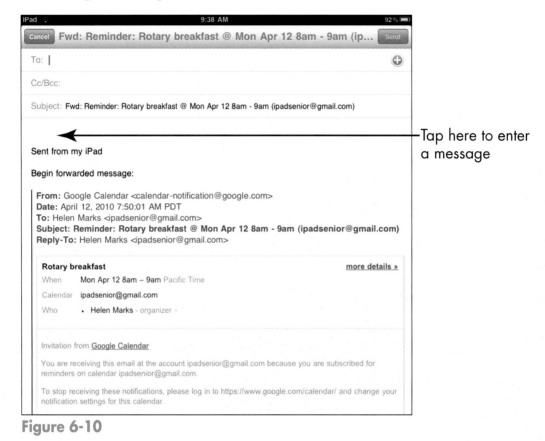

Figure 6-10

3. Tap Send. The message goes on its way.

Create and Send a New Message

1. With Mail open, tap the New Message icon. A blank message form (see **Figure 6-11**) appears.

2. Enter a recipient's address in the To field. If you have saved addresses in Contacts, tap the plus symbol in an address field to choose an addressee from the Contacts list.

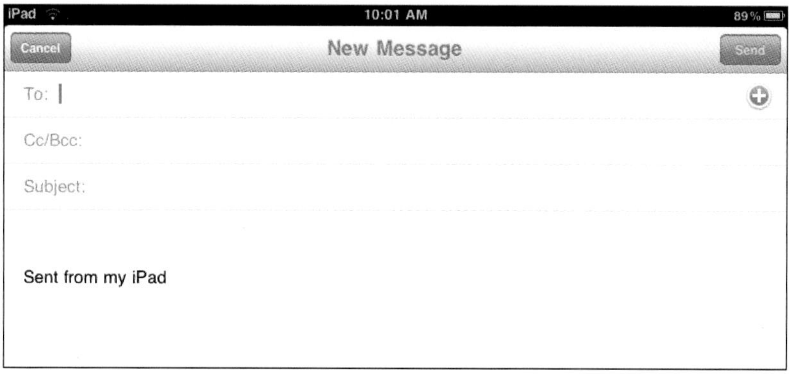

iPad	10:01 AM	89%
Cancel	New Message	Send

To: |

Cc/Bcc:

Subject:

Sent from my iPad

Figure 6-11

3. If you want to copy another person on the message, enter other addresses in the Cc/Bcc field. If you want to send both carbon copies and blind carbon copies, note that when you tap the Cc/Bcc field, two fields are displayed.

4. Enter a subject for the message in the Subject field.

5. Tap in the message body and type your message.

6. Tap Send.

 Mail keeps a copy of all sent messages. To view Sent messages, tap the Inbox button and then tap Mailboxes. Tap the Sent button and the folder containing all sent messages opens. Tap on a message to review it.

Search E-Mail

1. Say you want to find all messages from a certain person or with a certain word in the Subject field. You can use Mail's handy Search feature to find that e-mail. With Mail open, tap the Inbox button.

2. In the Inbox, shown in **Figure 6-12,** tap in the Search field. The on-screen keyboard appears.

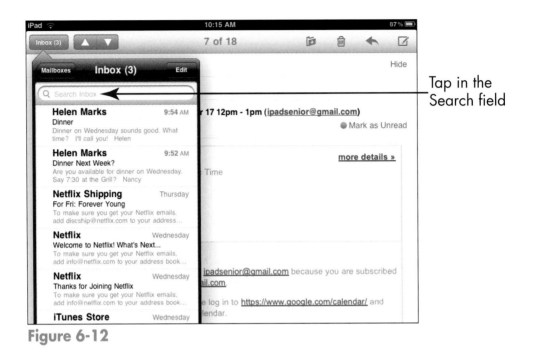

Tap in the Search field

Figure 6-12

3. Enter a search term or name.

4. Tap the From, To, or Subject tab to view messages that contain the search term in one of those fields, or tap the All tab to see messages in which any of these three fields contains the term. Matching e-mails are listed in the results, as shown in **Figure 6-13.**

 To start a new search or go back to the full Inbox, tap the Delete key in the upper-right corner of the on-screen keyboard to delete the term, or tap the Cancel button.

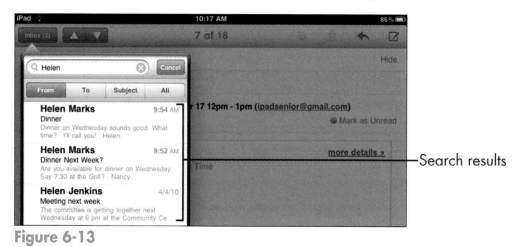

Figure 6-13 ——————Search results

Delete an E-Mail

1. When you no longer want an e-mail cluttering up your Inbox, you can delete it. With the Inbox displayed, tap the Edit button. Circular check boxes are displayed to the left of each message (see **Figure 6-14**).

2. Tap the circle next to the message you want to delete. You can tap multiple items if you have several e-mails to delete. Messages marked for deletion show a check mark displayed in the circular check box (refer to **Figure 6-14**).

3. Tap the Delete button. The message(s) is moved to the Trash folder.

 If you delete a message and then want to view it again, go to Mailboxes and then tap the Trash button. A list of deleted e-mails is displayed. If you want to retrieve one, you can move it back into the Inbox, using the procedure in the next task.

 You can also delete an open e-mail by tapping the trashcan icon in the toolbar that runs across the top.

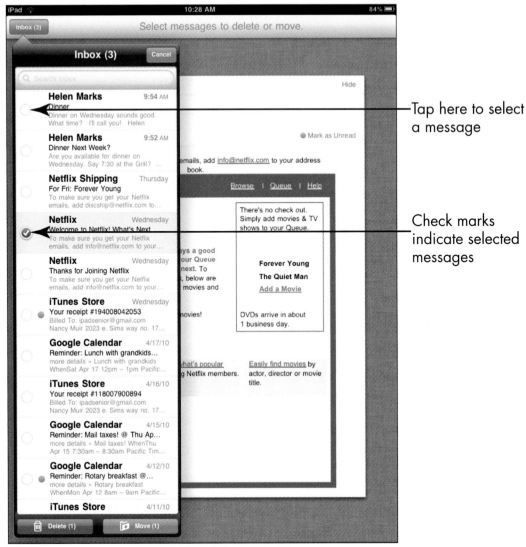

Tap here to select a message

Check marks indicate selected messages

Figure 6-14

Organize E-Mail

1. You can move messages into any of several pre-defined folders in Mail. With the folder containing the message you want to move (for example the Trash or Inbox) displayed, tap the Edit button. Circular check boxes are displayed to the left of each message (refer to **Figure 6-14**).

2. Tap the circle next to the message you want to move.

3. Tap the Move button.

4. In the Mailboxes list that appears (see **Figure 6-15**), tap the folder where you'd like to store the message. The message is moved.

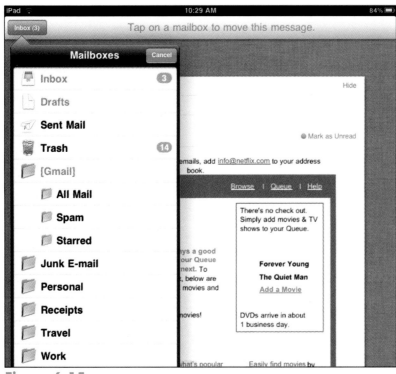

Figure 6-15

 If you get a junk e-mail, you might want to move it to the Spam folder. Once you do, any future mail from that same sender is automatically placed in the Spam folder.

 If you have an e-mail open, you can move it to a folder by tapping the Folder icon on the toolbar that runs along the top. The Mailboxes list displays; tap a folder to move the message.

Shopping the iTunes Store

*i*Pad is set up with an iTunes app that makes it easy to shop for music, movies, TV shows, audiobooks, podcasts, and even online classes at Apple's iTunes Store.

In this chapter, you find out how to use your iPad to open an iTunes account and find content on the iTunes Web site. That content can be downloaded directly to your iPad, or to your computer and then synced to your iPad. In addition, I cover a few options for buying content from other online stores.

Note that I cover opening an iTunes account and downloading iTunes software to your computer in Chapter 3. If you need to, go back to Chapter 3 and handle those two tasks before digging into this chapter.

Explore the iTunes Store

1. Using the iTunes Store from your iPad is easy with the built-in iTunes app. Tap the iTunes icon on the Home screen.

2. The dialog shown in **Figure 7-1** appears, asking for your iTunes password. Enter your password and tap OK.

Figure 7-1

3. Tap the Music button in the row of buttons at the bottom of the screen, if it's not already selected.

4. Tap the Next or Previous arrow to scroll through Featured selections, as shown in **Figure 7-2**.

5. Tap the Top Charts tab at the top of the screen. This displays top songs and albums.

6. Tap any of the other items listed to see more detail about them, as shown in **Figure 7-3**.

Tap these arrows to scroll through the selections

Figure 7-2

Jeff Healey					Artist Page >
Last Call					
Genre: Jazz					Tell a Friend >
Released: Apr 06, 2010					
14 Songs					
$9.99					

Tap to Preview

	Name	Time	Popularity	Price
1	Holding My Honey's Hand	2:59	‖‖‖‖‖‖	$0.99
2	Time On My Hands	5:02	‖‖‖‖‖‖	$0.99
3	The Wildcat	2:37	‖‖‖‖‖‖	$0.99

Figure 7-3

The navigation techniques in these steps work essentially the same in any of the content categories (the buttons at the bottom of the screen), which include Music, Movies, TV Shows, Podcasts, Audiobooks, and iTunesU. Just tap on one to explore it.

If you want to use the Genius playlist feature, which recommends additional purchases based on your previous purchases, turn this feature on in iTunes on your computer, and then on your iPad, tap the Genius tab. Song and album recommendations appear.

Find a Selection

There are several ways to look for a selection in the iTunes Store. You can use the Search feature, search by genres or categories, or view artists' pages. Here's how these work:

➡ Tap in the Search field shown in **Figure 7-4** and enter a search term using the on-screen keyboard. Tap the Search button on the keyboard or, if one of the suggestions given appeals to you, just tap on it.

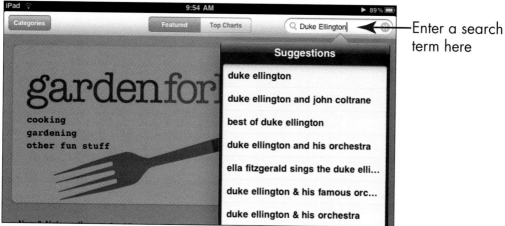

Enter a search term here

Figure 7-4

⇒ Tap the Genre button (in some content types, such as Audiobooks, this is called the Categories button). A list of genres/categories like the one shown in **Figure 7-5** appears.

Tap here to view the list

Figure 7-5

⇒ In a description page that appears when you tap a selection, you can find more offerings by people involved. For example, for a music selection, tap the Artist's Page link to see all of that artist's selections. For a movie, tap the name of someone in the movie credits to see more of that person's work, as shown for Kate Winslet in **Figure 7-6.**

Figure 7-6

 If you find a selection you like, tap the Tell a Friend link on its description page to share your discovery with a friend via e-mail. A message appears with a link to the selection. Enter an address in the To field and tap Send. Your friend is now in-the-know.

 Tap the See All link to see additional selections in a category or by an artist.

Sort Movie Selections

1. You can sort movie selections by best-sellers, name, or release date. With iTunes open, tap the Sort By field.

2. In the menu shown in **Figure 7-7,** tap the criteria you want to sort by.

Figure 7-7

3. Selections are sorted by the criteria you chose (for example, alphabetically if you chose Name or with the latest release first if you chose Release Date).

Preview Music, a Movie, or an Audiobook

1. Because you have already set up an iTunes account (if you haven't done so yet, refer to Chapter 3), when you choose to buy an item it's automatically charged to the credit card you have on record. You might want to preview an item before you buy it. If you like it, buying and downloading are then easy and quick. Open iTunes and locate a selection you might want to buy using any of the methods outlined in earlier tasks.

2. Tap the item to see detailed information about it, as shown in **Figure 7-8.**

Patsy Cline			Artist Page >	
Patsy Cline's Greatest Hits				
(Remastered)			Tell a Friend >	
Genre: Country				
Released: 1967				
12 Songs				
★★★★★ 61 Ratings				
$9.99				

iTunes Review

Considering her legendary status, it's amazing that Patsy Cline only recorded 104 tracks over a span of eight years. Her ability to convey romantic torment without ever losing her grace or dignity remains unmatched, and for those looking for the essence of Cline's music, *Greatest* ...   More ▼

Tap to Preview

	Name	Time	Popularity	Price
1	Walkin' After Midnight (1961 Remake)	1:59		$1.29
2	Sweet Dreams (Single Version)	2:33		$0.99
3	Crazy (Single Version)	2:41		$1.29

Tap a track number or name to listen to a preview

Figure 7-8

3. If you're looking at a music selection, tap the track number or name of a selection (refer to **Figure 7-8**) to play a preview. For a movie or Audiobook selection, tap the Preview button shown in **Figure 7-9**.

 The iTunes Store offers several free selections, especially in the Podcast and iTunesU content categories. If you see one you'd like to try out, download it by tapping the button labeled Free and then tapping the Get Episode or similar button that appears.

The Blind Side [PG-13]   Tell a Friend >

Warner Bros.   Language: English
Genre: Drama   Format: Widescreen
Released: 2010   Dolby Digital 5.1 surround sound
Run Time: 2:08:31
☆☆☆☆☆ 2325 Ratings

                                PREVIEW

Tap here to preview the selection

RENT $4.99   HD   Standard Def.

Learn About Rentals >

iTunes Extras

Includes a one-on-one "Sideline Conversation" with Sandra Bullock and more. Enjoy them on your Mac, PC, or Apple TV. iTunes Extras are available with purchase only.

Plot Summary

Sandra Bullock, Tim McGraw and Oscar® winner Kathy Bates star in this remarkable true story of All-American football star Michael Oher. Teenager Michael Oher (Quinton Aaron) is surviving on his own, virtually homeless, when he is spotted on the street by Leigh Anne Tuohy (Sa... **More ▼**

Bonus Content:
If you purchase this movie, the next time you connect to the iTunes Store on your computer you will also receive:
▥ iTunes Extras - The Blind Side

Credits

Actors	Director	Screenwriter	Producers
Sandra Bullock >	John Lee Hancock >	John Lee Hancock >	Gil Netter >
Tim McGraw >			Broderick Johnson >

Figure 7-9

Buy a Selection

1. When you find an item you want to buy, tap the button that shows either the price (if it's a selection available for purchase; see **Figure 7-10**) or the word Free (if it's a selection available for free).

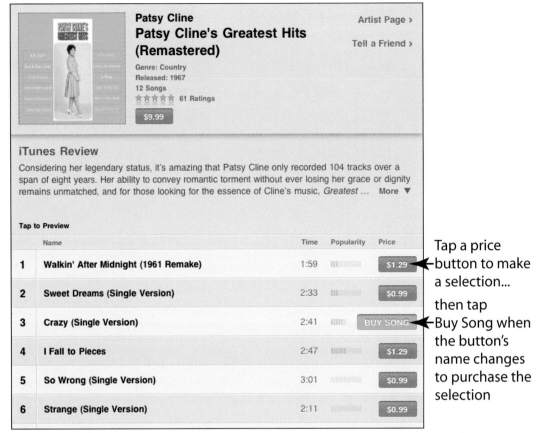

Tap a price button to make a selection...

then tap Buy Song when the button's name changes to purchase the selection

Figure 7-10

2. The button label changes to Buy X, where X is the type of content you're buying (refer to **Figure 7-10**).

3. Tap the Buy X button. The iTunes Password dialog appears (refer to **Figure 7-1**).

4. Enter your password and tap OK. The item begins downloading (see **Figure 7-11**) and is automatically charged to your credit card. When the download finishes, you can view the content using the iPod or Video app, depending on the type of content.

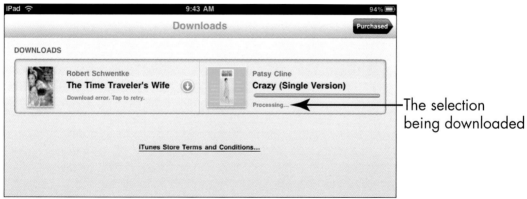

The selection being downloaded

Figure 7-11

 If you want to buy music, you can open the description page for an album and buy individual songs rather than the entire album. Tap on the price for a song, and then proceed to purchase it.

 Note the Redeem button on many iTunes screens. Tap this button to redeem any iTunes gift certificates you might get from your generous friends, or from yourself.

Rent Movies

1. In the case of movies, you can either rent or buy content. If you rent, which is less expensive, you have 30 days from the time you rent the item to begin to watch it. Once you have begun to watch it, you have 24 hours from that time left to watch it as many times as you like. With iTunes open, tap the Movies button.

2. Locate the movie you want to rent and tap the View button shown in **Figure 7-12**.

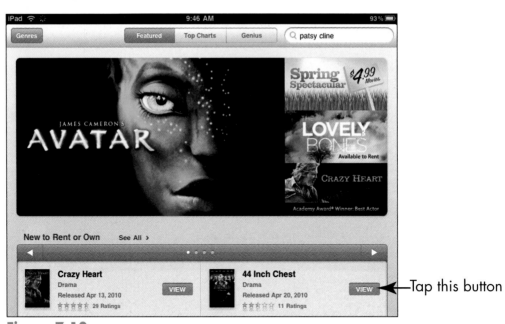

Tap this button

Figure 7-12

3. In the detailed description of the movie that appears, tap the Rent button shown in **Figure 7-13.**

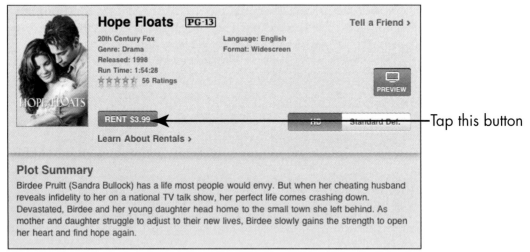

Tap this button

Figure 7-13

4. The gray Rent button changes to a green Rent Movie button; tap it to confirm the rental. The movie begins to download to your iPad immediately and the credit card associated with your account is charged the rental fee.

5. To check the status of your download, tap the Downloads button. The progress of your download is displayed. Once the download is complete, you can use either the iPod or Videos app to watch it. (See Chapters 10 and 12 to read about how these apps work).

 Some movies are offered in high-definition versions. These HD movies will look great on that crisp, colorful iPad screen.

 You can also download content to your computer and sync it to your iPad. Refer to Chapter 3 for more about this process.

Listen to Podcasts

1. *Podcasts* are audio broadcasts you can listen to on your iPad. Most of these are free and feature a wide variety of topics. With iTunes open, tap the Podcast button in the row of buttons at the bottom of the screen.

2. Tap on a Podcast selection; a detailed listing of podcasts like the one shown in **Figure 7-14** appears.

3. Tap on the name or number of a podcast for a preview, or simply tap the Free button, and then tap the Get Episode button (refer to **Figure 7-14**) to download the podcast. Once it downloads, you can play it using the iPod app.

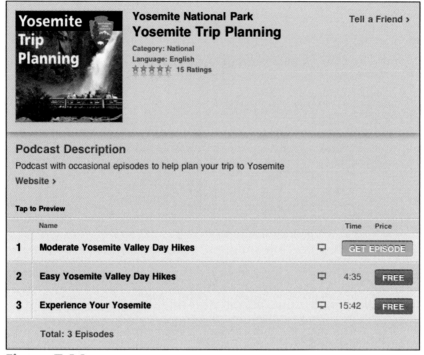

Yosemite National Park
Yosemite Trip Planning

Tell a Friend >

Category: National
Language: English
★★★★☆ 15 Ratings

Podcast Description

Podcast with occasional episodes to help plan your trip to Yosemite

Website >

Tap to Preview

	Name		Time	Price
1	Moderate Yosemite Valley Day Hikes	🖵		GET EPISODE
2	Easy Yosemite Valley Day Hikes	🖵	4:35	FREE
3	Experience Your Yosemite	🖵	15:42	FREE
	Total: 3 Episodes			

Figure 7-14

Go to School at iTunes U

1. One very cool feature of iTunes is *iTunes U*, a compilation of free online courses from universities and other providers. Tap the iTunes U button in the row of buttons at the bottom of the screen to display selections.

2. Tap one of the three tabs shown in **Figure 7-15**: Universities & Colleges, Beyond Campus, or K-12.

3. On the list that appears, tap an item to select the source for a course. That provider's page appears.

4. Tap the Next or Previous button to scroll through offerings. When you find a topic of interest, tap a selection and it opens, displaying a list of segments of the course as shown in **Figure 7-16**.

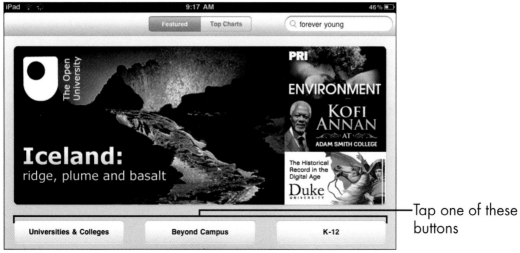

iPad
9:17 AM
46%
Featured
Top Charts
forever young
The Open University
Iceland:
ridge, plume and basalt
PRI
ENVIRONMENT
KOFI ANNAN
AT
ADAM SMITH COLLEGE
The Historical Record in the Digital Age
Duke
UNIVERSITY
Universities & Colleges
Beyond Campus
K-12
Tap one of these buttons

Figure 7-15

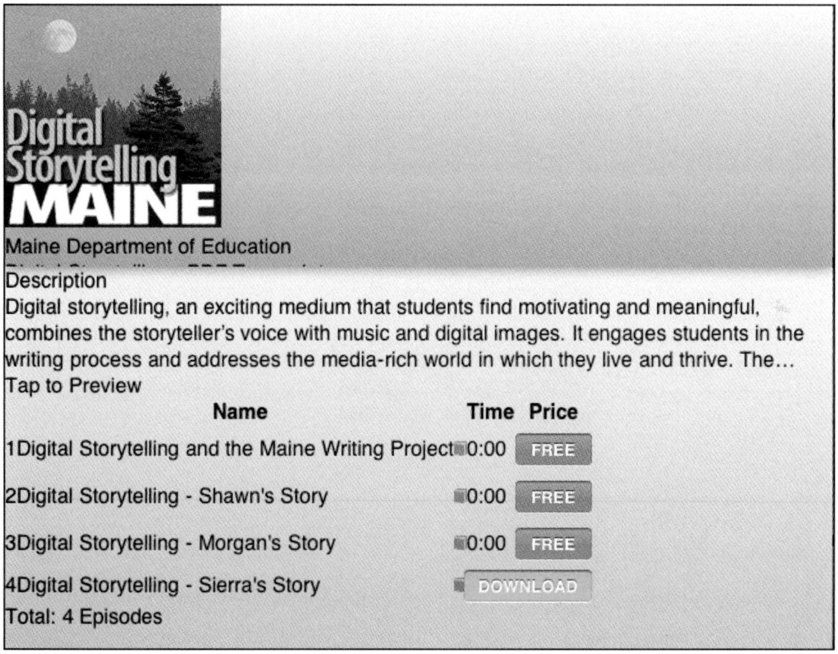

Digital Storytelling MAINE
Maine Department of Education
Description
Digital storytelling, an exciting medium that students find motivating and meaningful, combines the storyteller's voice with music and digital images. It engages students in the writing process and addresses the media-rich world in which they live and thrive. The...
Tap to Preview
Name
Time
Price
1Digital Storytelling and the Maine Writing Project
0:00
FREE
2Digital Storytelling - Shawn's Story
0:00
FREE
3Digital Storytelling - Morgan's Story
0:00
FREE
4Digital Storytelling - Sierra's Story
DOWNLOAD
Total: 4 Episodes

Figure 7-16

5. Tap the Free button next to a course, and then tap the green Download button that appears. The course begins downloading.

Once you're on a provider's page, to return to iTunesU, just tap the back button labeled iTunes U (located in the upper-left corner of the screen) and you return to the page with the three provider tabs (refer to **Figure 7-15**).

Shop Anywhere Else

One feature that's missing from iPad is support for Flash, a format of video playback that many online video-on-demand services use. However, many content stores are hurriedly adding iPad-friendly videos to their collections, so you do have options to iTunes for your choice of movies or TV shows.

You can open accounts at these stores by using your computer or your iPad's Safari browser and then following a store's instructions for purchasing and downloading content.

Here are some of the stores that are offering iPad-compatible content, with more coming all the time:

➡ Clicker.com

➡ UStream.com

➡ ABC and CBS news

➡ Netflix.com

Expanding Your iPad Horizons with Apps

Some apps (short for applications) come pre-installed on your iPad, such as Contacts and Videos. But there's a world of other apps out there that you can get for your iPad, some for free, such as iBooks, and some for a price (typically from 99 cents to about ten dollars).

Apps range from games to financial tools and productivity applications, such as the iPad version of Pages, the Apple word processing software.

In this chapter, I suggest some apps you might want to check out and explain how to use the App Store feature of iPad to find, purchase, and download apps.

Get ready to . . .

Explore Senior-Recommended Apps

As I write this book, apps are being furiously created for iPad, so this list won't be exhaustive by the time you have this book in your hands. Still, I want to provide a quick list of some apps that might whet your appetite to get you exploring what's out there.

Access the App Store by tapping the App Store icon on the Home screen and then check these apps out:

⟼ **Sudoku** (Free; see **Figure 8-1**): If you like this mental math puzzle in print, try it out on your iPad. There are several levels ranging from easy to hard, making this a great way to make time fly by in the doctor or dentist's waiting room.

⟼ **Stocks Portfolio for iPad:** Keep track of your investments on your iPad with this app. You can use it to create a watch list and record your stock performance.

⟼ **Price Grabber for iPad:** Use this app to find low prices on just about everything. Read product reviews and compare list prices.

⟼ **FlickrStackr:** If you use Flickr photo sharing service on your computer, why not bring the same features to your iPad? This is a great app for sharing images with family and friends.

⟼ **Paint Studio:** Get creative! You can use this powerful app to draw, add color, and even create special effects. If you don't need all those features, try Paint Studio Jr.

⟼ **Pocket Weather World HD:** Get weather reports wherever you are over your iPad. This app includes more than 60,000 locations worldwide.

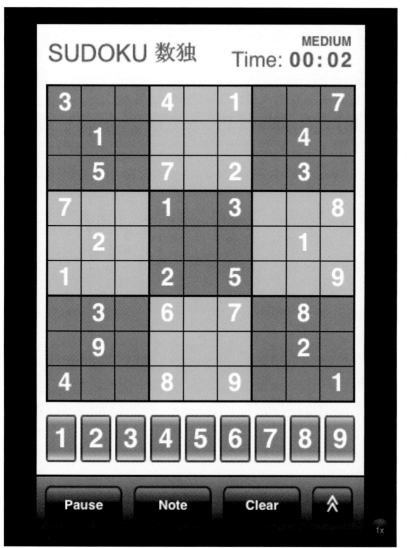

Figure 8-1

⟩⟩ **Mediquations Medical Calculator:** Use this handy utility to help you calculate medications with built-in formulas and read scores for various medications. Check with your physician before using!

 iBooks is the great, free eReader app that opens up a world of reading on your iPad. See Chapter 9 for details about using iBooks.

Most iPhone apps will work on your iPad, so if you own the pricey mobile phone and have favorite apps on it, sync them to your iPad!

Search the App Store

1. Tap the App Store icon on the Home screen. The site shown in **Figure 8-2** appears.

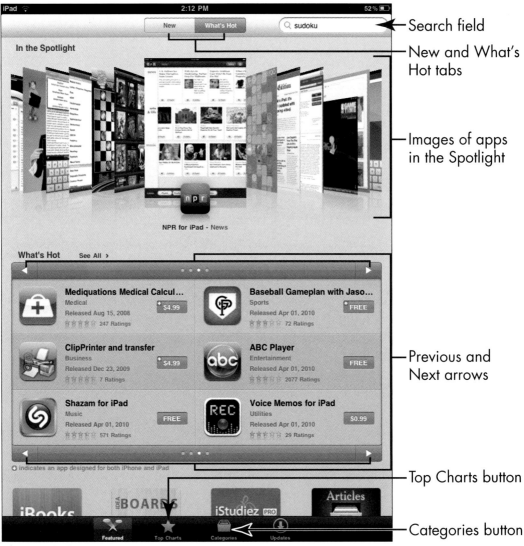

Search field

New and What's Hot tabs

Images of apps in the Spotlight

Previous and Next arrows

Top Charts button

Categories button

Figure 8-2

2. At this point, you have several options for finding apps:

- Tap in the Search field, enter a search term, and tap the Search button on the on-screen keyboard to see results.

- Tap the Previous or Next arrow to see more selections, or tap the See All link to display all selections.

- Tap one of the images of an app in the Spotlight area at the top of the screen to see more details about it.

- Tap the New or What's Hot tab at the top of the screen to see those categories of apps.

- Tap the Top Charts button on the bottom of the screen to see what free and paid apps other people are downloading most.

- Tap the Categories button to search by types of apps, as shown in **Figure 8-3**.

Figure 8-3

Get Applications from the App Store

1. Buying apps requires that you have an iTunes account, which I cover in Chapter 3. Once you have an account, you can use the saved payment information there to buy apps with a few simple steps, or download free apps. I strongly recommend you install the free iBooks app, and I walk you through getting it here. With the App Store open, tap the Search field and enter iBooks.

2. Tap on the Free button for iBooks in the results that appear, as shown in **Figure 8-4**. (Note that, to get a paid app, you'd tap on the Price button at this point.)

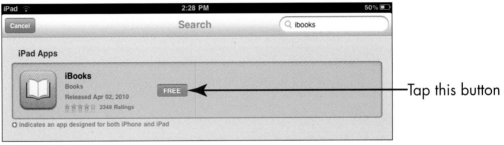

Tap this button

Figure 8-4

3. The Free button changes to read Install App (or, in the case of a paid app, the button changes to read Buy App). Tap that button; you may be asked to enter your iTunes password and tap the OK button to proceed.

4. The app downloads; if you purchase an app that isn't free, at this point your credit card is charged for the purchase price.

 Only pre-installed apps are located on the first Home screen. Apps you download are placed on additional Home screens, and you have to scroll to view and use them unless you move them to the Dock and from there to a different Home screen. See the next task for help in finding your newly downloaded apps using multiple Home screens.

Organize Your Applications

1. iPad can display up to 11 Home screens. By default, the first contains pre-installed apps; other screens are created to contain any apps you download or sync to your iPad. At the bottom of the original iPad Home screen (just above the Dock), a magnifying glass icon represents the Search screen to the left of the primary Home screen; dots that appear indicate how many screens there are and which Home screen you are on at the moment, as shown in **Figure 8-5**. Tap the Home button to open the last displayed Home screen.

Dots inticating the number of screens

Magnifying glass icon | The screen you're currently on

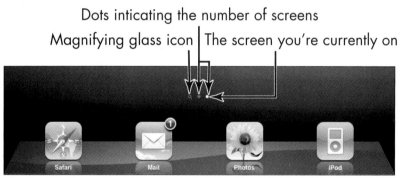

Figure 8-5

2. Flick your finger from right to left to move to the next Home screen. Note that the dots near the bottom of the screen indicate which Home screen you're on.

3. To reorganize apps on a Home screen, press and hold any app on that page. The app icons begin to jiggle (see **Figure 8-6**).

4. Press, hold, and drag an app icon to another location on the screen to move it.

5. Tap the Home button to stop all those icons from jiggling!

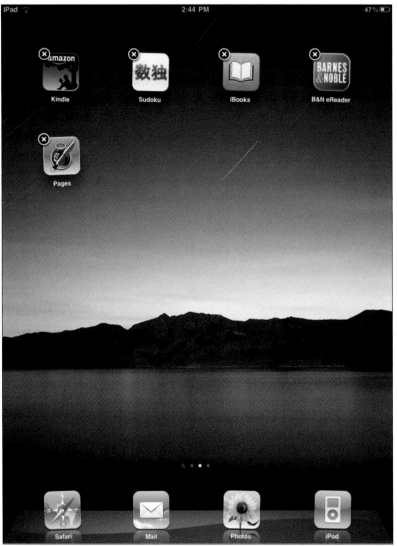

Figure 8-6

To move an app from one page to another, while things are jiggling, you can press, hold, and drag an app to the Dock. Apps on the Dock are available on every Home screen. If you want to then move an app on the Dock you can move it to any Home screen when in jiggle mode.

Delete Applications You No Longer Need

1. When you no longer need an app that you have installed, it's time to get rid of it. (You can't delete apps that come automatically with iPad.) Display the Home screen that contains the app you want to delete.

2. Press and hold the app until all apps begin to jiggle.

3. Tap the Delete button for the app you want to delete (see **Figure 8-7**).

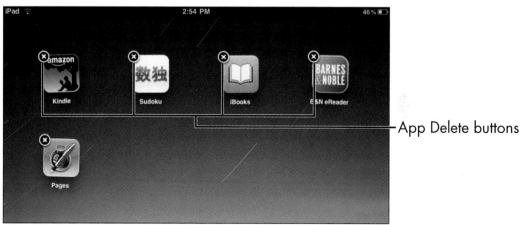

Figure 8-7

4. The confirmation shown in **Figure 8-8** appears. Tap OK to proceed with the deletion.

Figure 8-8

5. A dialog asking you to rate an app before deleting it appears after Step 4; you can tap the Rate button to rate it or No Thanks to opt out of the survey.

Part III

Having Fun and Consuming Media

The 5th Wave — By Rich Tennant

©RICHTENNANT

Accessories

iPadPad

"It's a docking system for the iPad that comes with 3 bedrooms, 2 baths, and a car port."

Using Your iPad as an eReader

A traditional eReader is a device that is used to read electronic versions of books, magazines, and newspapers. Apple has touted iPad as a great eReader, so, though it isn't a traditional eReader device like Amazon's Kindle, you won't want to miss out on this very cool functionality.

Apple's free, downloadable application that turns your iPad into an eReader is called *iBooks*. iBooks enables you to buy and download books from Apple's iBookstore. There are also several other free eReader applications, such as Kindle, Stanza, and Barnes & Noble's eReader, that you can use to download books to your iPad from a variety of online bookstores and read to your heart's content.

In this chapter, you discover the options available for reading material and how to buy books. You also learn all about iBooks: how to navigate a book and adjust the brightness and type, as well as how to search books and organize your iBooks library.

Get ready to . . .

Discover How iPad Differs from Other eReaders

An *eReader* is any electronic device that enables you to download and read books, magazines, and newspapers. These devices are typically dedicated only to reading electronic versions of books, are very portable, and most use technology called eInk to create a paperlike reading experience.

The iPad is a bit different: It isn't only for reading books and you have to download an application to enable it as an eReader (though the application is free). Also, it doesn't offer the paperlike reading experience — you read from a computer screen (though you can adjust the brightness of that screen).

When you buy a book or magazine online (or get one of many free publications), it downloads to your iPad in a few seconds using a Wi-Fi or 3G connection. iPad offers several navigation tools to move around a book, which you explore in this chapter.

Find Books at iBooks

1. In Chapter 8, I walk you through the process of downloading the iBooks application in the "Get Applications from the App Store" task, so you should go back and do that first if you haven't already. To shop using iBooks, tap on the iBooks application icon to open it. (Note that it is probably located on your second Home screen, so you may have to swipe your finger to the left on the Home screen to locate it.)

2. In the iBooks library that opens (see **Figure 9-1**), you see a bookshelf; yours probably has only one free book already downloaded to it. (If you don't see the bookshelf, tap the Library button to go there or, if no Library button is on the screen, tap the Bookshelf button at the top-right corner of the screen — it sports four small squares.) Tap the Store button and the shelf pivots around 180 degrees.

Tap the Store button

Figure 9-1

3. In the iBookstore shown in **Figure 9-2,** do any of the following to find a book:

- Tap the Search field and type a search word or phrase using the on-screen keyboard.

- Tap the right or left arrows located in the middle of the screen to scroll to more suggested titles.

- Tap the Categories button to see a list of types of books, as shown in **Figure 9-3.** Tap on a category to view those selections.

- Tap See All to view more titles.

- Tap the appropriate button at the bottom of the screen to view Featured titles, the New York Times Bestseller List, books listed on Top Charts, or Purchases to review the titles you've already purchased.

- Tap on a suggested selection or featured book ad to open more information about it.

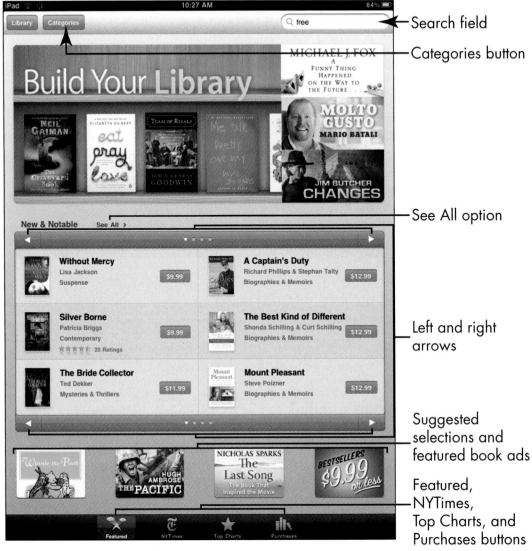

Figure 9-2

 Download free samples before you buy. You get to read several pages of the book to see if it appeals to you, and it doesn't cost you a dime! Look for the Get Sample button when you view details about a book.

Figure 9-3

Explore other eBook Sources

iPad is capable of reading book content from other bookstores, so you can get books from sources other than iBookstore. To do so, first download another eReader application such as Kindle from Amazon or the Barnes & Noble reader from the iPad App Store (see Chapter 8 for how to download apps). Then use their features to search for, purchase, and download content.

The Kindle eReader application is shown in **Figure 9-4.** Any content you have already bought from Kindle is archived online and can be placed on your Kindle Home page in iPad for you to read any time you like. Deleting an application from this reader works the same as for iBooks: Just swipe a title toward the right and the Delete button appears.

Figure 9-4

Buy Books

1. If you have set up an account with iTunes, you can buy
books at the iBookstore easily (see Chapter 3 for more
about setting up an account). When you find a book in
the iBookstore that you'd like to buy, tap its Price button.
The button changes to a Buy Book button, as shown in
Figure 9-5.

Tap a Price button...

and it changes to a Buy Book button

Figure 9-5

2. Tap the Buy Book button. The iTunes Password dialog shown in **Figure 9-6** appears.

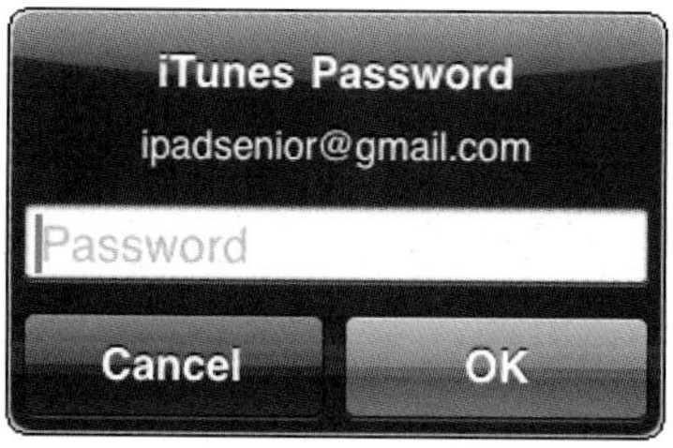

Figure 9-6

3. Enter your password and tap OK.

4. The book appears on your bookshelf, and the cost has been charged to whatever credit card you provided when you opened your iTunes account.

You can also sync books you've downloaded to your computer to your iPad using the data connection cord and your iTunes account. Using this method, you can find lots of free books from various sources online and drag them into your iTunes audiobook library; then simply sync them to your iPad. See Chapter 3 for more about syncing.

Navigate a Book

1. Tap iBooks and if your Library (the bookshelf) isn't already displayed, tap the Library button.

2. Tap a book to open it. The book opens, as shown in **Figure 9-7**. (If you hold your iPad in portrait orientation, it shows one page; if in landscape orientation, it will show two).

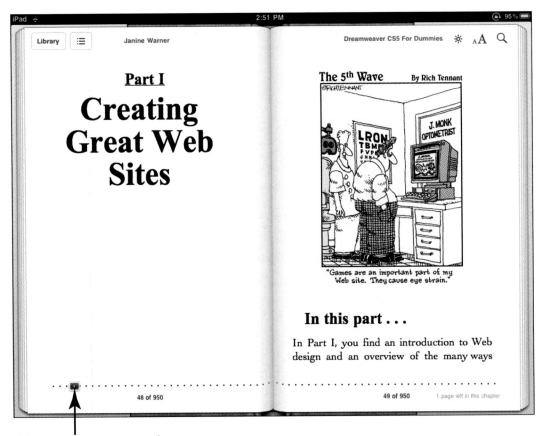

Slider to move to another page

Figure 9-7

3. Take any of these actions to navigate through the book:

- Tap and drag the slider at the bottom of the page to the right or left to move to another page in the book.

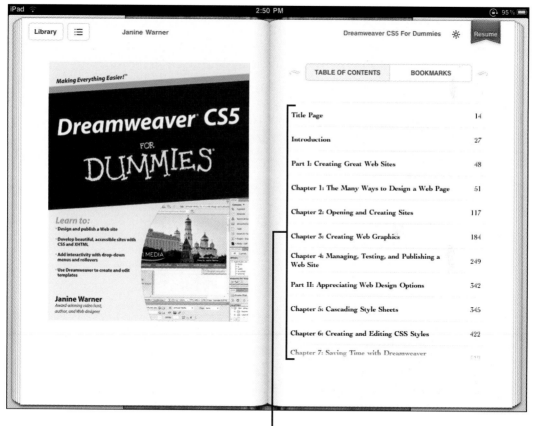

- Tap the Table of Contents button at the top of the page (it looks like a little bulleted list) to go to the book's Table of Contents (see **Figure 9-8**) and then tap on a chapter to go to it.

Tap any chapter to go to it

Figure 9-8

- Place your finger on the bottom-right corner of a page and flick it to the left to turn to the next page.

- Place your finger on the bottom-left corner of a page and flick it to the right to turn to the preceding page.

 To return to the Library to view another book at any time, tap the Library button. If the button isn't visible, press your finger near the top of the screen and the toolbar appears.

Adjust Brightness

1. iBooks offers an adjustable brightness setting that you can use to make your book pages comfortable for you to read. With a book open, tap the Brightness button shown in **Figure 9-9**.

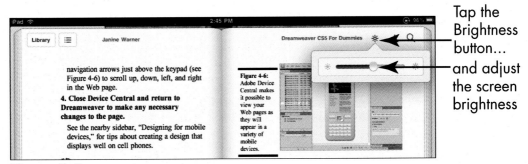

Tap the Brightness button...

and adjust the screen brightness

Figure 9-9

2. In the Brightness dialog that appears (refer to **Figure 9-9**), tap and drag the slider to the right to make the screen brighter, or to the left to dim the screen.

3. Tap anywhere in the book to close the Brightness dialog.

 You'll have to experiment with the brightness that works for you. It's commonly thought that bright white computer screens are hard on the eyes, so going with the halfway default setting or below is probably a good idea.

Change the Font Size and Type

1. If the type on your screen is a bit small for your taste, you can change to a larger font size, or choose a different font for readability. With a book open, tap the Font button (it sports a small and a large capital A, as shown in **Figure 9-10**).

Tap the Font button to change font size and type

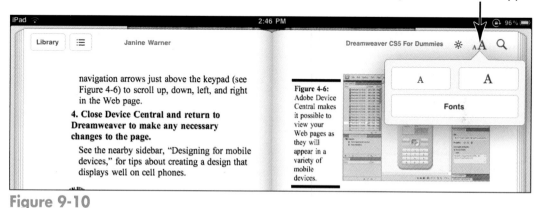

Figure 9-10

2. In the Font dialog that appears (refer to **Figure 9-10**), tap the A button on the left to use smaller text, or the A button on the right to use larger text.

3. Tap the Fonts button. The list of fonts shown in **Figure 9-11** appears.

4. Tap on a font name to select it. The font changes on the book page.

5. Tap outside the Fonts dialog to return to your book.

 Some fonts appear a bit larger on your screen than others because of their design. If you want the largest fonts, use Cochin or Verdana.

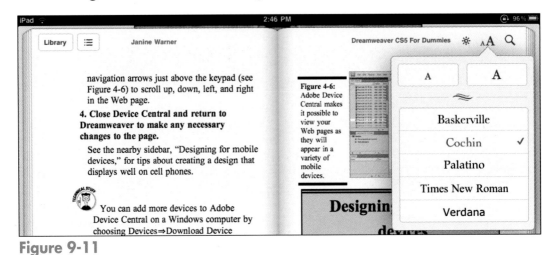

Figure 9-11

Search in Your Book

1. You may want to find a certain sentence or reference in your book. To do so, with the book displayed, tap the Search button shown in **Figure 9-12**. The on-screen keyboard displays.

2. Enter a search term and then tap the Search key on the keyboard. iBooks searches for any matching entries.

3. Use your finger to scroll down the entries (see **Figure 9-13**).

4. If you wish, you can use the Search Google or Search Wikipedia buttons at the bottom of the Search dialog to search for information about the search term online.

 You can also search for other instances of a particular word while in the book pages by pressing your finger on the word and tapping Search in the toolbar that appears.

The Search button

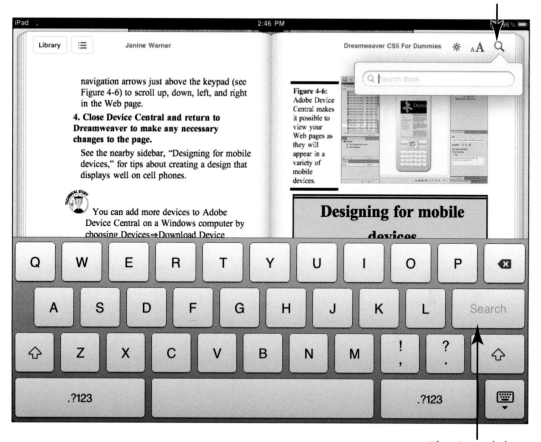

The Search key

Figure 9-12

Scroll through the entries

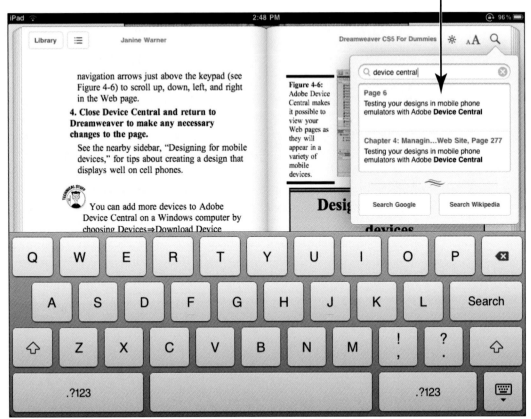

Figure 9-13

Use Bookmarks

1. Bookmarks in your eBooks are like favorites you save in your Web browser: They enable you to revisit a favorite passage or refresh your memory about a character or plot point. With a book open, press on a word until the toolbar shown in **Figure** 9-14 appears.

2. Tap the Bookmark button. A colored highlight is placed on the word.

3. To change the color of the bookmark or remove it, tap the bookmarked word. The toolbar in **Figure** 9-15 appears.

Tap this button

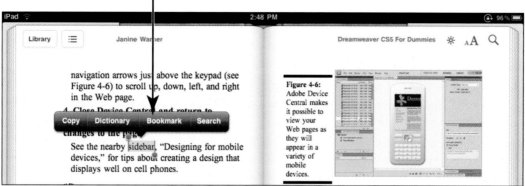

Figure 9-14

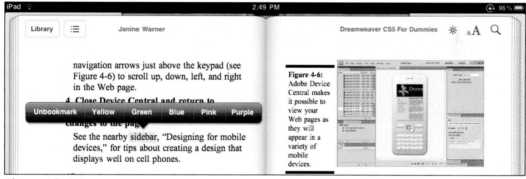

Figure 9-15

4. Take one of two actions:

- Tap another color button to change the bookmark color.

- Tap the Unbookmark button to remove the bookmark.

5. Tap outside of the bookmark to close the toolbar.

6. To go to bookmarks, tap the Table of Contents button on a book page.

7. In the Table of Contents, tap the Bookmarks tab. As shown in **Figure 9-16,** all bookmarks are displayed.

Bookmarks are displayed here

Figure 9-16

8. Tap on a bookmark in this list to go there.

 iPad automatically bookmarks where you left off reading in a book so you don't have to do that manually.

 You can also bookmark illustrations in a book. Display the page and press on the image until the Bookmark button appears above it. Tap the button, and the illustration gets a colored border. As with bookmarked text, you can tap on a bookmarked illustration to change the highlight color or unbookmark it.

Check Words in the Dictionary

1. As you read a book, you may come across unfamiliar words. Don't skip over them — take the opportunity to learn a word! With a book open, press your finger on a word and hold it until the toolbar shown in **Figure 9-17** appears.

Tap this button

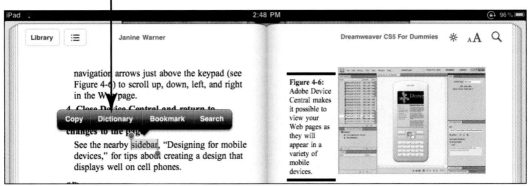

Figure 9-17

2. Tap the Dictionary button. A definition dialog appears, as shown in **Figure 9-18**.

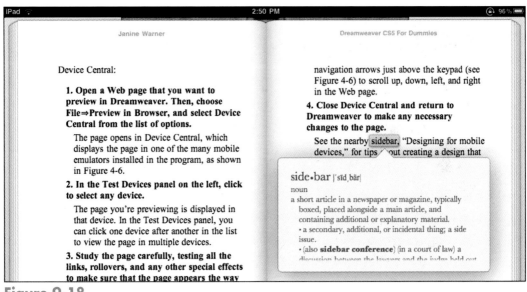

Figure 9-18

3. Tap the definition and scroll down to view more.

4. When you finish reviewing the definition, tap anywhere on the page and the definition disappears.

Organize Your Library

1. Your library looks like a bookshelf with books stored on it, with the most recently downloaded title in the top-left corner. However, if you prefer, you can view your library in a few other ways. With the bookshelf version of the library displayed, tap the List button shown in **Figure 9-19**.

List button

Figure 9-19

2. Your books appear in a list, as shown in **Figure 9-20**. To organize the list alphabetically by Titles or Authors, tap the appropriate button on the bottom of the screen.

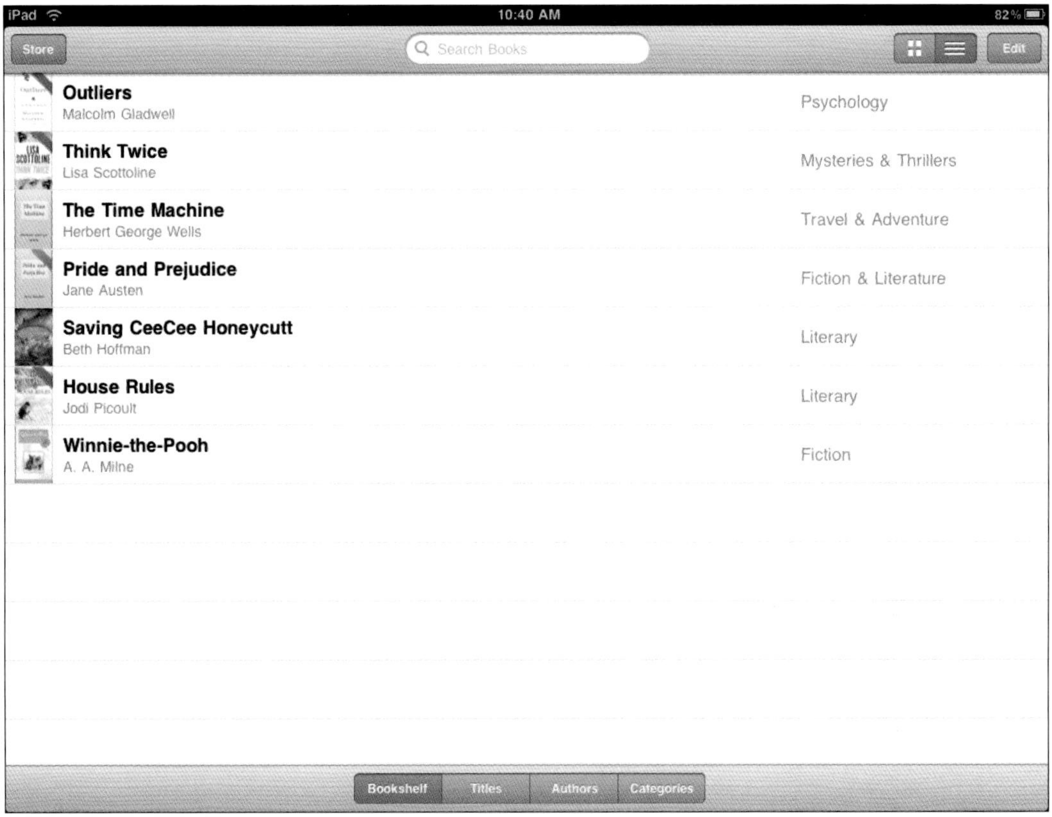

Figure 9-20

3. To organize by categories, tap the Categories button. Your titles are divided by category titles such as Fiction, Mysteries & Thrillers, or Literary, as shown in **Figure 9-21.**

iPad 🖥	11:29 AM	78% 🔋

Store | 🔍 Search Books | ⊞ ≡ Edit

Fiction

Winnie-the-Pooh
A. A. Milne
Fiction

Fiction & Literature

Pride and Prejudice
Jane Austen
Fiction & Literature

Literary

House Rules
Jodi Picoult
Literary

Saving CeeCee Honeycutt
Beth Hoffman
Literary

Mysteries & Thrillers

Think Twice
Lisa Scottoline
Mysteries & Thrillers

Psychology

Outliers
Malcolm Gladwell
Psychology

Travel & Adventure

The Time Machine
Herbert George Wells
Travel & Adventure

Bookshelf | Titles | Authors | Categories

Figure 9-21

 4. To return to the bookshelf view at any time, tap the Bookshelf view button.

 The Bookshelf button in the list view displays the bookshelf order, which lists the most recently down-loaded book first.

Use the Edit button in the list view to display Delete buttons for all books in the list. Tap the book-specific Delete buttons (which look like minus signs) to delete books, and then tap the Done button to exit the Edit function.

Playing Music with the iPod App

Chapter
10

*Y*ou've probably heard of the iPod — a small, portable, music-playing device from Apple that's seemingly glued into the ears of many kids and teens. iPad includes an iPod app that allows you to take advantage of its pretty amazing little sound system to play your own style of music or podcasts and audio-books. You can also play movies with the iPod app (though the Videos app provides a few more features, so you might prefer it to iPod, whose specialty is music).

In this chapter, you get acquainted with the iPod app and its features that allow you to sort and find music and control playback.

Get ready to . . .

View the Library Contents

1. Tap the iPod app icon located in the Dock on the Home screen. The iPod Library appears (see **Figure 10-1**).

Figure 10-1

2. Tap the Music, Podcasts, or Audiobooks button in the left panel of the Library to open one of these collections (see **Figure 10-2**).

Tap a button to view the collection

Figure 10-2

3. Tap the Purchased button in the Library to view all the items you've purchased, including videos, podcasts, music, and audiobooks.

 iTunes has several free items you can download and use to play around with the features in iPod, including music, podcasts, and audiobooks. You can also sync content stored on your computer to your iPad and play it using iPod. See Chapter 3 for more about syncing and Chapter 7 for more about getting content from iTunes.

Sort by Songs, Artists, and More

1. To view music by a variety of criteria, first tap iPod on the Home screen to open it.

2. Tap the buttons along the bottom of the screen to sort music by these self-explanatory categories:

- Songs

- Artists

- Albums

- Genres (see **Figure 10-3**)

- Composers

 It's kind of fun to tap the Composers tab and see who wrote the music you seem to prefer. With the Composers panel displayed, tap an album/song link to connect the composer with the songs he or she wrote. You might be surprised who wrote your favorite songs!

 You can create your own playlists to put tracks from various sources into collections of your choosing. Tap the plus sign in the bottom-left corner of the iPad screen, and enter a name for the playlist in the New Playlist dialog that appears. Tap Save, and then in the list of selections that appears, tap the plus sign next to each item you'd like to include. Tap the Done button, then tap Done again on the list that appears. Your playlist appears in the Library list and you can now play it by tapping the list name and then the Play button.

Tap a category button to sort the collection

Figure 10-3

Search for Audio

1. You can search for an item in your iPod library using the Search feature. With iPod open, tap in the Search field. The on-screen keyboard opens, as shown in **Figure 10-4**.

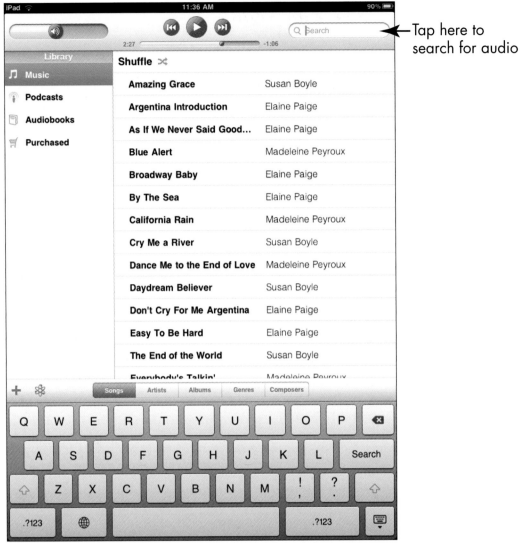

Tap here to
search for audio

Figure 10-4

2. Enter a search term in the Search field. Results are displayed, narrowing down as you type, as shown in **Figure 10-5.**

3. Tap an item to play it.

 You can enter an artist's name, author's/composer's name, or a word from the item's title in the Search field to find what you're looking for.

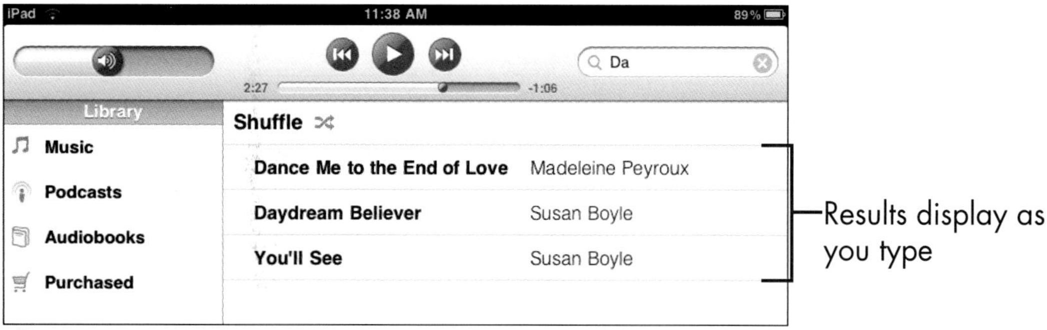

Figure 10-5

Play Music and Other Audio

1. Locate the song, podcast, or audiobook you want to play using the methods described in previous tasks.

2. Tap the album, podcast, or audiobook that contains the item you want to play. Note that if you are displaying the Songs tab or the Purchased library, you don't have to tap an album to open a song; you need only tap on a song to play it.

3. Tap the item you want to play from the list that appears (see **Figure 10-6**); it begins to play.

4. Use the Previous and Next buttons at the top of the screen shown in **Figure 10-7** to navigate the audio file that's playing. The Previous button actually takes you back to the beginning of the item that's currently playing; the Next button takes you to the next item.

5. Tap the Pause button to pause playback.

6. Tap and drag the circle that indicates the current playback location on the Progress bar left or right to "scrub" to another location in the song.

Tap an item to play it

Figure 10-6

7. Don't like what's playing? Tap the Back to Library arrow in the bottom-left corner to return to the Library view, or tap the Album List button in the bottom-right corner to show other selections in the currently playing album and make another selection.

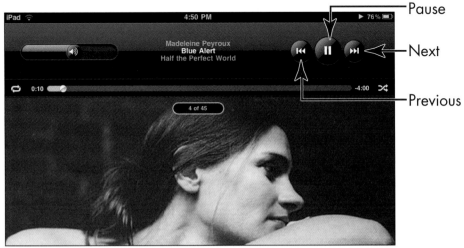

Pause

Next

Previous

Figure 10-7

If you play a song on an album, the album cover displays full screen. To close it and return to your iPod library, place two fingers on the screen and pinch them inward.

 You can use the Genius Playlist feature in iTunes to set up playlists of recommended content in your iPad Library. Based on items you've purchased, iTunes suggests other purchases that would go well with your collection. Okay, it's a way to get you to buy more music, but if you are building your music collection, it might be worth a try! Visit the iTunes site at www.apple.com/itunes for more information.

Shuffle Music

1. If you'd like to play a random selection of the music you've purchased or synced from your computer, you can do that using the Shuffle feature. With iPod open, tap either the Music or Purchased button in the library pane on the left and then tap the Songs button on the bottom of the screen.

2. Tap the Shuffle button (see **Figure 10-8**). Your content plays in random order.

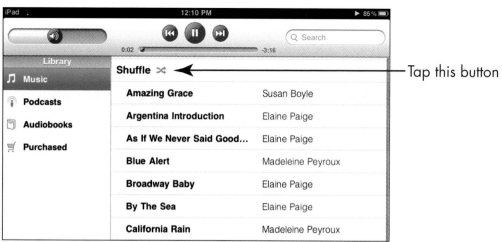

Figure 10-8

In the Purchased collection of your library, all media is displayed. If you shuffle you might find TV shows, movies, and podcasts playing here and there. If you just want music, tap the Music collection before tapping Shuffle.

Adjust the Volume

1. iPod offers its own volume control that you can adjust during playback. With iPod open, tap on a piece of music, podcast, or audiobook to play it.

2. In the controls that display (see **Figure 10-9**), press and drag the button on the Volume slider to the right for more volume or to the left for less volume.

iPad	12:21 PM	83%

Use the Volume slider to adjust the volume

Library
🎵 Music
Podcasts
Audiobooks
🛒 Purchased

Podcasts — UNSEEN

UNSEEN: Spain
● UNSEEN
29:51   4/14

Get More Episodes...

Figure 10-9

 If you've got volume set at high and you're still having trouble hearing, consider getting a headset. These cut out extraneous noises and may improve the sound quality of what you're listening to. You'll need a 3.5-mm stereo headphone; insert it in the headphone jack on the top of your iPad.

Playing with Photos

With its gorgeous screen, iPad is a natural for viewing photos. iPad supports most common photo formats, such as JPEG, TIFF, PNG, and GIF. You can get your photos from your computer, iPhone, or digital camera. You can also save images you find online to your iPad.

When you have photos to play with, the Photos app allows you to view them in albums, one-by-one, or in a slideshow. You can also e-mail a photo to a friend or use your expensive gadget as an electronic picture frame, all of which you read about in this chapter.

Import Photos from a Digital Camera or iPhone

1. You can find information about syncing your computer with your iPad to port over photos in Chapter 3. However, your computer isn't the only photo source available to you. You can also import photos from a digital camera or iPhone if you buy the iPad Camera Connection Kit from Apple. The iPad Camera Connection Kit contains two adapters (see **Figure 11-1**): a USB Camera Connector you use to import photos from a digital camera or iPhone, and an SD Card Reader to import from an SD card. Start the import process by locking your iPad.

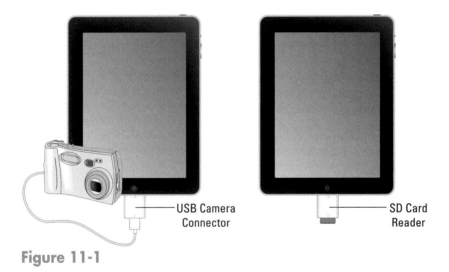

USB Camera
Connector

SD Card
Reader

Figure 11-1

2. Insert the USB Camera Connector into the Dock connector slot of your digital camera or iPhone.

3. Connect the USB end of the cord that came with your digital camera or iPhone into the USB Camera Connector.

4. Connect the other end of the cord that came with your camera or iPhone into that device.

5. Unlock your iPad. The Photos app opens and displays the photos on the digital camera or iPhone.

6. Tap Import All on your iPad; if you only want to import selected photos, tap individual photos and then tap Import. Finally, tap Import rather than Import All. The photos are saved to the Last Import album.

7. Disconnect the cord and the adapter and you're done!

 You can also import photos stored on an *SD* (secure digital) memory card often used by digital cameras as a storage medium. Simply lock the iPad, insert the SD Card Reader into the iPad, insert the SD card containing the photos, and then follow Steps 5–7 above.

Save Photos from the Web

1. The Web offers a wealth of images that you can download to your Photo Library. Open Safari and navigate to the Web page containing the image you want.

2. Press and hold the image; a menu appears, as shown in **Figure 11-2**.

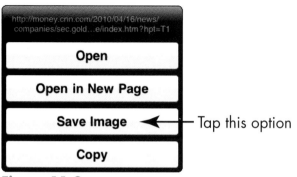

Figure 11-2

3. Tap Save Image. The image is saved to your Saved Photos album in the Photos app, as shown in **Figure 11-3.**

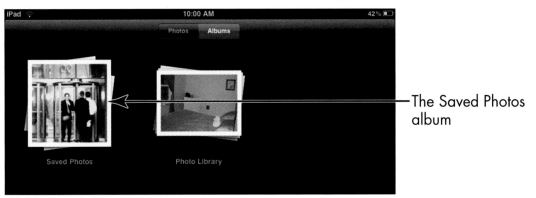

The Saved Photos album

Figure 11-3

 For more about how to use Safari to navigate to or search for Web content, see Chapter 5.

View an Album

1. The Photos app organizes your pictures into albums. The Saved Photos album contains images you save from the Web and screenshots you take of your iPad screen (do this by pressing the Sleep/Wake and Home buttons at the same time). The Photo Library album stores images you import from your computer. There may also be albums for images you synced from devices such as your iPhone or digital camera. To view albums, tap the Photos app icon in the Dock on the Home screen.

2. If the Photos tab is selected when the Photos app opens, tap the Albums tab shown in **Figure 11-4.**

3. Tap an album. The photos in it are displayed, as shown in **Figure 11-5.**

Tap this tab to
view albums

Figure 11-4

Figure 11-5

 Photos doesn't offer the option of creating new
albums and moving pictures among albums, a regret-
table omission in this first version of iPad that may
be improved on in later versions.

View Individual Photos

1. Tap the Photos app icon in the Dock on the Home screen.

2. Tap the Photos tab (shown in **Figure 11-6**).

iPad   12:17 PM   53%

Photos   —Tab this tab

Laptops For Seniors DUMMIES

Figure 11-6

3. To view a photo, pinch your fingers together, place them on the photo, and then spread your fingers apart. The picture expands, as shown in **Figure 11-7**.

4. Flick your finger to the left or right to scroll through the individual photos in that album.

5. To reduce the size of the individual photos and return to the multi-picture view, place two fingers on the photo and then pinch them together.

 You can place a photo on a person's information page in Contacts. For more about how to do this, see Chapter 15.

Figure 11-7

Share Photos

1. It's easy to share photos stored on your iPad by sending them as e-mail attachments. First, tap the Photos app icon in the Dock on the Home screen.

2. Tap the Photos tab, and locate the photo you want to share.

3. Tap on the photo to select it, and then tap the Sharing icon (it looks like a box with an arrow jumping out of it). The menu shown in **Figure 11-8** appears.

4. Tap the Email Photo option.

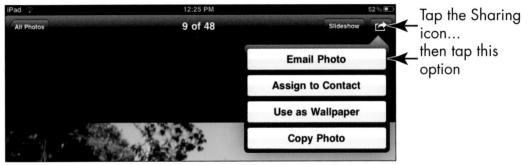

Tap the Sharing icon...

then tap this option

Figure 11-8

5. In the e-mail message form that appears (see **Figure 11-9**), make any modifications you wish in the To, Cc/ Bcc, or Subject fields. You can also tap within the body of the message and add more text.

Figure 11-9

6. Tap the Send button and the message and photo go on their way.

 You can also copy and paste a photo into documents such as those created in the available Pages word processor application. To do this, press and hold a photo in Photos until the Copy command appears. Tap Copy, and then in the destination application, press and hold the screen and tap Paste.

Run a Slideshow

1. You can run a slideshow of your images in Photos and even play music and choose transition effects for the show. Tap the Photos app icon to open the application.

2. Tap the Photos tab.

3. Tap the Slideshow button to see the Slideshow Options menu, shown in **Figure 11-10**.

Figure 11-10

4. If you want to play music along with the slideshow, tap the On/Off button on the Play Music field.

5. To choose the music that will play along with the slide-show, tap the Music field and in the list that appears (see **Figure 11-11**), tap any selection from your iPod library.

Figure 11-11

6. Tap the transition effect you want to use for your slide-show (refer to **Figure 11-10**).

7. Tap the Start Slideshow button. The slideshow begins.

 To run a slideshow that includes only the photos contained in a particular album, tap the Album tab, tap an album to open it, and then tap the Slideshow button to make settings and run a slideshow.

Display Picture Frame

1. You can use the slideshow settings you created in the previous task to run your slideshow while your iPad screen is locked so you can view a continuous display of your pictures. Tap the Sleep/Wake button to lock iPad, and then tap the Home button to go to the lock screen; the bottom of this screen looks like **Figure 11-12.**

The Picture Frame button

Figure 11-12

2. Tap the Picture Frame button (refer to **Figure 11-12**). The slideshow begins (see **Figure 11-13**). To end the show, tap the Home button.

 If you don't like the effects used on the picture frame, go back to Photos and change the slideshow settings.

Figure 11-13

Delete Photos

1. You might find it's time to get rid of some of those old photos of the family reunion or the last community center project. If those photos weren't transferred from your computer but instead were downloaded or captured as screenshots on the iPad, you can delete them. Tap the Photos app icon in the Dock on the Home screen.

2. Tap the Albums tab and then tap the Saved Photos album to open it.

3. Tap an individual photo to open it.

4. Tap the Trash Can button, and then tap the Delete Photo button that appears, as shown in **Figure 11-14**.

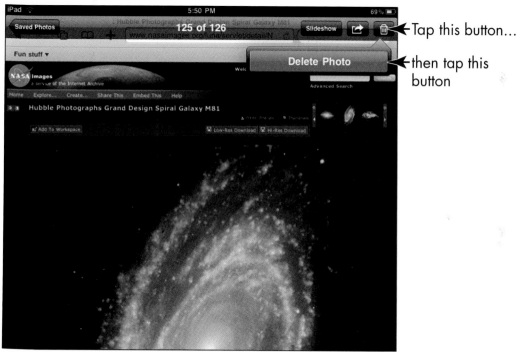

Figure 11-14

Watching Videos and YouTube

You have two built-in applications on your iPad that focus on viewing videos. The Videos app is a player with which you can watch downloaded movies or TV shows or media you've synced from your Mac or PC. The YouTube app takes you online to the popular video-sharing site. Videos here range from professional music videos to clips from news or entertainment shows and personal videos of cats dancing and news-making events.

In this chapter, I explain how to use controls in both apps to play programs and how to use some of the YouTube features to rate, share, and save favorite videos. You might want to refer to Chapter 7 first to purchase or download one of many free TV shows or movies you can practice with.

Chapter 12

Get ready to . . .

Play Movies, Podcast, or TV Shows with Videos

1. Tap the Videos app icon on the Home screen to open the application.

2. In the screen like the one shown in **Figure 12-1**, tap the Movies, Podcast, or TV Shows tab, depending on which you want to watch.

Tap the Movies or TV Show tab

Figure 12-1

3. Tap on an item to open it. A description appears, as shown in **Figure 12-2**.

The Play button

Figure 12-2

4. Tap the Play button. The movie, podcast, or TV show opens and begins playing. Note that the progress of the playback is displayed on the top of the screen, showing how many minutes you've viewed and how many remain (see **Figure 12-3**). If you don't see this, tap the screen once and it will display briefly along with a set of playback tools at the bottom of the screen.

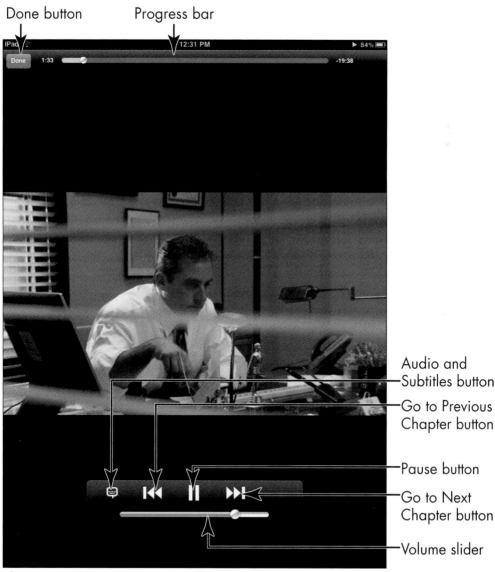

Done button   Progress bar

Audio and Subtitles button

Go to Previous Chapter button

Pause button

Go to Next Chapter button

Volume slider

Figure 12-3

5. With the playback tools displayed, take any of the following actions:

- Tap the Pause button to pause playback.

- Tap Go to Previous Chapter or Go to Next Chapter to move to a different location in the video playback.

- Tap the circular button on the Volume slider and drag it left or right to decrease or increase the volume, respectively.

6. To stop the video and return to the information screen, tap the Done button.

 Note that if you've watched a video before and stopped partway through, it opens to the last spot you were viewing by default. To start a video from the beginning, tap and drag the circular button on the Progress bar all the way to the left.

 You can connect iPad to your television so you can watch videos on the more vision-friendly larger screen. To do this, you have to buy either an Apple iPad Dock or a VGA Connector cable at the Apple Store as well as have any other appropriate cables for your TV to complete the connection.

Turn on Closed Captioning

1. iTunes and iPad offer support for closed captioning and subtitles. If a movie you purchased or rented has either closed captioning or subtitles, you can turn on the feature in iPad. Begin by tapping the Settings icon on the Home screen.

2. On the screen that appears (see **Figure** 12-4), tap Video in the Settings section on the left-hand side of the screen.

Tap Video...

then tap here to turn on Closed Captioning

Figure 12-4

3. In the menu that displays on the right-hand side of the screen (refer to **Figure** 12-4), tap the Closed Captioning On/Off button to turn the feature on. Now when you play a movie with closed captioning, you can click the Audio and Subtitles button to the left of the playback controls to manage these features.

Go to a Movie Chapter

1. Tap the Videos app icon on the Home Screen.

2. Tap on the Movie tab if it isn't already displayed.

3. Tap on the movie you want to watch. Information about the movie is displayed, as shown in **Figure** 12-5.

Figure 12-5

4. Tap the Chapters tab. A list of chapters is displayed, as shown in **Figure 12-6**.

5. Tap on a chapter to play it.

 You can also use the playback tools to go back one chapter or forward one chapter. See the "Play Movies or TV Shows with Videos" task, earlier in this chapter, for more information.

Tap this tab...

to view the list of chapters

Figure 12-6

Delete an Item from iPad

1. Tap the Videos app icon on the Home screen.

2. Locate the item you want to delete on the Movies, Podcasts, or TV Shows tab.

3. Press and hold the item; a Delete button appears, as shown in **Figure 12-7**.

The Delete button

Figure 12-7

4. Tap the Delete button. The item is deleted.

If you buy a video using iTunes, download it to your iPad, and then delete it from iPad, it's still saved in your iTunes library. You can sync your computer and iPad again to download it once more. However, rented movies, once deleted, are gone with the wind.

iPads have much smaller storage capacity than your typical computer, so downloading lots of TV shows or movies can fill that storage up quickly. If you don't want to view an item again, delete it to free up space.

Find Videos on YouTube

1. Though you can go to YouTube and use all its features using iPad's Safari browser, it's easier using the dedicated YouTube application that's built in to iPad when you buy it. This version features buttons you can tap to display different content and features using your touch-screen. Tap the YouTube app icon on the Home screen to open it.

2. Tap the Featured button at the bottom of the screen if it's not already selected (see **Figure 12-8**).

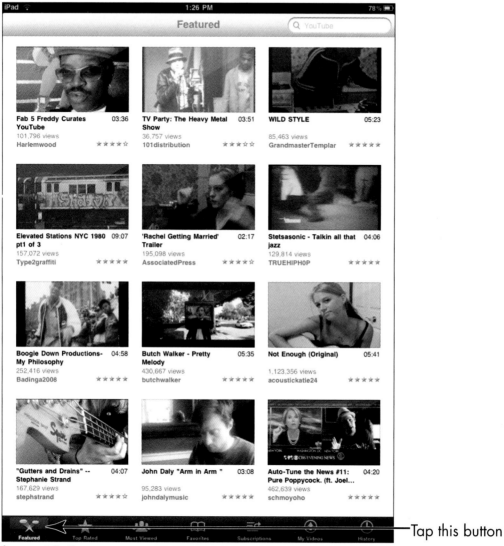

Tap this button

Figure 12-8

3. To find videos you'd like to watch, tap in the Search field. The keyboard opens, as shown in **Figure 12-9**.

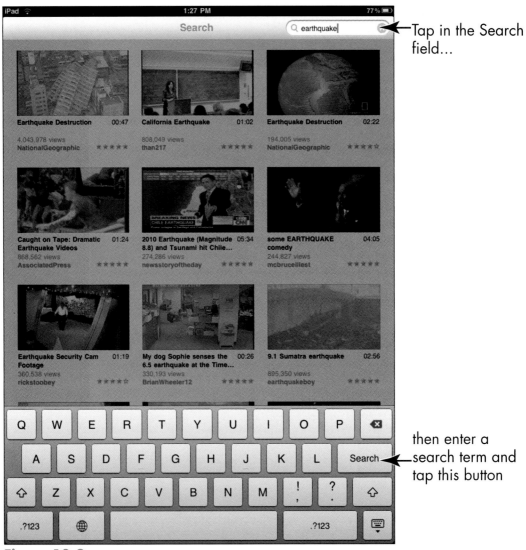

Tap in the Search field...

then enter a search term and tap this button

Figure 12-9

4. Type a search term and tap the Search button on the keyboard (refer to **Figure 12-9**).

5. Use your finger to scroll down the screen to see additional results.

6. To display the top-rated or most-viewed videos, tap the Top Rated or Most Viewed button on the bottom of the screen.

7. When you find a movie you want to view, tap it to display it. The movie begins loading (see **Figure 12-10**). See the next task for details of how to control the playback.

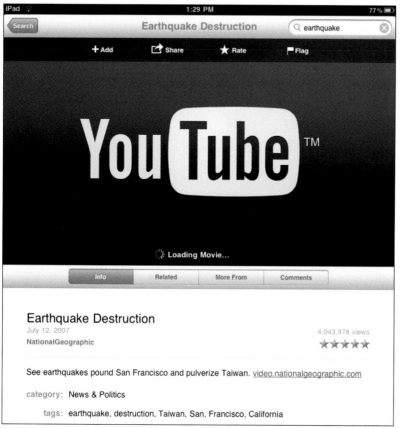

Figure 12-10

 When you load a movie, you can use the Related and More From tabs in the playback window (refer to **Figure 12-10**) to find additional content related to the topic, or more videos posted on YouTube by the same source.

 If you find a movie you like, tap the More From tab and you can then tap the Subscribe button to subscribe to all movies from this source. View your subscriptions by tapping the Subscriptions button at the bottom of the YouTube screen.

Control Video Playback

1. With a video displayed (see the previous task), tap the Play button. The video plays, as shown in **Figure 12-11**.

Play/Pause button

Playback progress bar

Figure 12-11

2. Tap the Pause button to pause playback. (If the button is not visible, tap the screen in the black area on either side of the video once to display it.)

3. To move forward or backward in the movie, tap the circular button on the Playback progress bar and drag it right or left.

 When the video is finished, you can replay it from the beginning by tapping the Play button again.

Change Views

1. In the previous task, you watched a video in the smallest of three available views. To change to larger views, tap the Play button and then tap the Full Screen button. The video displays in a full screen version with a black border, as shown in **Figure 12-12**.

Figure 12-12

 2. To go to an even larger view, tap the button in the top-right corner. The movie fills the screen, as in **Figure 12-13**.

3. To reduce the movie back to its smallest size, tap the button on the right side of the playback controls. Tap the button in the upper right-hand corner to return to the medium view.

Figure 12-13

 You can use the double-tap method of enlarging the playback when in either of the two larger screen formats. Double-tapping the smaller of the two moves you to the largest full screen view. Double-tapping the largest full screen view zooms in further. Depending on the quality of the video, the largest zoom factor could produce a rather grainy image.

Flag Content as Inappropriate

1. If there's a chance your grandkids could get ahold of your iPad, you might appreciate the capability to flag inappropriate content on YouTube. First you have to set a Restriction in your YouTube account using your computer, and then set a flag using the iPad YouTube app, which causes a passcode to be required to access that content. With a video open in the YouTube application, tap in the black area near the top of the screen to display tools, as shown in **Figure 12-14.**

Display this toolbar

Figure 12-14

2. Tap the Flag option.

3. Tap the Flag As Inappropriate button that appears (see **Figure 12-15**).

Tap this option...

then tap
this button

Figure 12-15

Rate Videos

1. Display a video you want to rate.

2. Tap the Rate button shown in **Figure 12-16**.

Tap the Rate
button...

then tap the
desired number
of stars

Figure 12-16

3. Tap the number of stars you want in the Rate field that appears (refer to **Figure 12-16**) to rate the video (1 is the lowest rating, 5 the highest).

 Remember that you can view the highest rated videos on YouTube by tapping the Top Rated button at the bottom of the screen.

Share Videos

1. Display a video you want to share.

2. Tap the Share button shown in **Figure 12-17**.

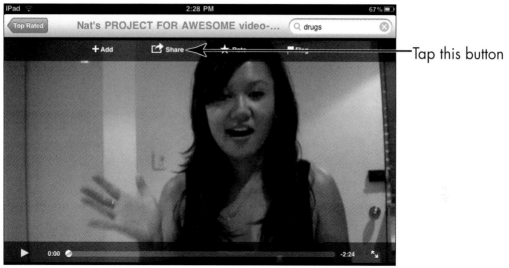

Tap this button

Figure 12-17

3. In the e-mail form shown in **Figure 12-18**, enter a recipient in the To field and add to the message if you like.

Figure 12-18

4. Tap the Send button to send a link to the video.

 If you like a movie enough to share it, you might also be interested in the Comments feature. With a video displayed, tap the Comments tab. Tap in the Add a Comment field, type your comment, and tap the Send button on your keyboard. Your comment is posted.

Add to Video Favorites

1. Display a video you want to add to Favorites.

2. Tap the Add button shown in **Figure 12-19**.

3. In the menu shown (refer to **Figure 12-19**), tap Favorites.

4. To view your favorite movies, tap the Favorites button at the bottom of the YouTube screen. Your favorite videos are displayed (see **Figure 12-20**).

 To delete a favorite while in the Favorites screen, tap the Edit button. Delete buttons appear on each movie. Tap the movie-specific Delete button to remove that movie. Tap the Done button to leave the editing mode.

—Tap this button...

—then tap Favorites

Figure 12-19

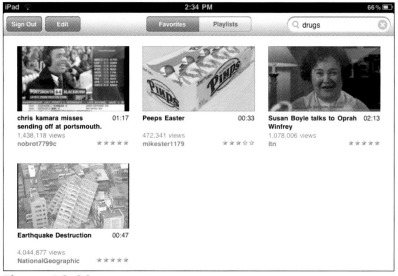

Figure 12-20

Finding Your Way with Maps

*I*f you own an iPhone, the Google Maps app on iPad will be very familiar. The big difference with iPad is the large screen you have to view all the beautiful map visuals and new terrain and street views.

If you're new to the Maps app, there are lots of great functions in it. You can get directions from one location to another. You can bookmark locations to return to them again. And the Maps app makes it possible to get information about locations, such as the phone numbers and Web links to businesses. You can even look at a building or location as if you were standing in front of it on the street, add a location to your Contacts list, or e-mail a location link to your buddy.

Be prepared: This is a seriously cool application, and you're about to have lots of fun exploring it in this chapter.

Get ready to . . .

Go to Your Current Location

1. iPad can figure out where you are at any point in time and display your current location. From the Home screen, tap the Maps icon. Tap the Current Location icon (the small circle to the left of the Search field; see **Figure 13-1**).

Current Location icon

Figure 13-1

2. Your current location is displayed with a blue pin and a blue circle around it (refer to **Figure 13-1**). The circle indicates how accurate the location is — it could actually be anywhere within the area of the circle, and is likely to be less accurate with a Wi-Fi–only iPad.

3. Double-tap the screen to zoom in on your location. (Additional methods of zooming in and out are covered in the "Zoom In and Out" task, later in this chapter.)

 If you don't have a 3G version of iPad, your current location is a rough estimate based on a triangulation method. Only 3G-enabled iPads with GPS can really pinpoint where you are. Still, if you type in a starting location and an ending location to get directions, you can get pretty accurate results even with a Wi-Fi–only iPad.

Change Views

1. The Maps application offers four views: Classic, Satellite, Hybrid, and Terrain. You view the Classic view by default the first time you open Maps. To change views, with Maps open, swipe the bottom-right corner of the screen to turn the "page" and reveal the Maps menu shown in **Figure 13-2**.

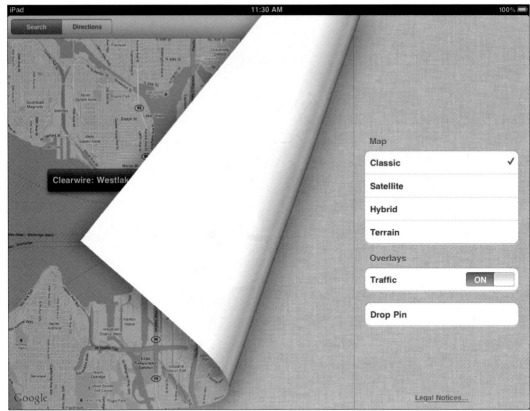

Figure 13-2

2. Tap the Satellite option and flick the corner of the page to fold it back. The Satellite view shown in **Figure 13-3** appears.

Figure 13-3

3. Swipe to reveal the menu again and tap Hybrid. This displays a Satellite view with street names superimposed, as shown in **Figure 13-4**.

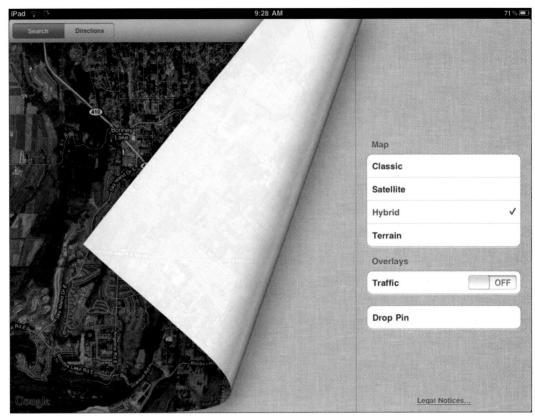

Figure 13-4

4. Finally, swipe to reveal the menu one more time and tap
Terrain. A topographical version of the map is displayed
(see **Figure 13-5**), showing hills, mountains, and valleys.
This is very helpful if you want to walk around San
Francisco and avoid those steep streets!

 On the Maps menu you'll also see a Traffic overlay
feature. If you live in a congested area, turn this feature on by tapping the On/Off button. Traffic overlay
shows different colors on roads indicating accidents
or road closures to help you navigate your rush-hour
commute or trip to the mall. Green means you're
good to go, yellow indicates slowdowns, and red
means avoid at all costs.

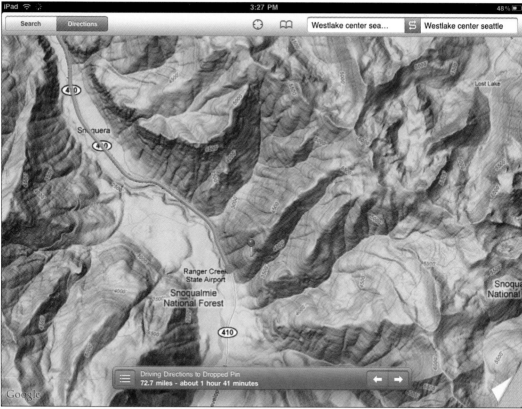

Figure 13-5

 You can drop a pin to mark a location on a map that you can return to. See the task "Drop A Pin," later in this chapter, for more about this.

Zoom In and Out

1. You'll appreciate this application because it gives you the capability to zoom in and out to see more or less detailed maps and to move around a displayed map. With a map displayed, double-tap with a single finger to zoom in (see **Figure 13-6**).

2. Double-tap with two fingers to zoom out, revealing less detail (see **Figure 13-7**).

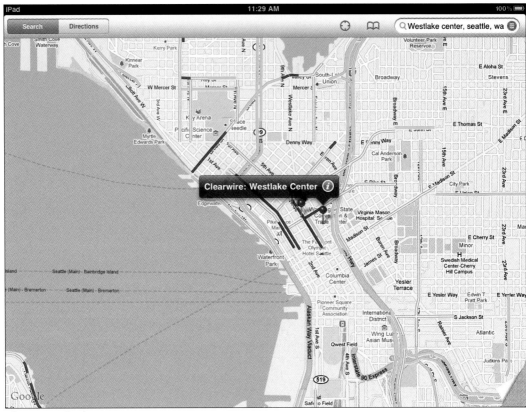

Figure 13-6

_3._ Place two fingers positioned together on the screen and move them apart to zoom in.

_4._ Place two fingers apart on the screen and then pinch them together to zoom out.

_5._ Press your finger to the screen, and drag the map in any direction to move to an adjacent area.

 It can take a few moments for the map to redraw itself when you enlarge, reduce, or move around it, so try a little patience. Areas that are being redrawn will look like a blank grid, but will fill in, in time. Also, if you're in Satellite view, zooming in may take some time; wait it out, because the blurred image will resolve itself.

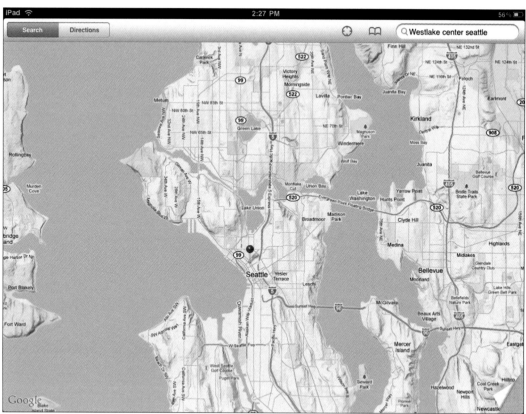

Figure 13-7

Go to Another Location

1. With Maps open, tap in the Search field; the keyboard opens (see **Figure 13-8**).

2. Type a location, using a street address with city and state, or a destination such as Empire State Building or Detroit Airport. Maps may make suggestions as you type if it finds any logical matches. Tap the Search button and the location appears with a red pin inserted in it and a label with the location, an Information icon, and in some cases, a Street view icon (see **Figure 13-9**). Note that if several locations match your search term, several pins may be displayed.

Tap in the Search field...

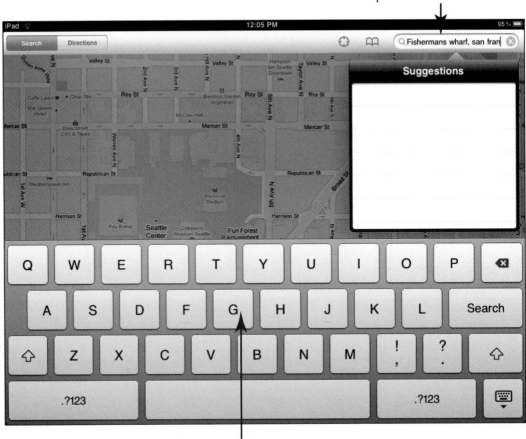

then type a location

Figure 13-8

3. You can also tap the screen and drag in any direction to move to a nearby location.

4. Tap the Bookmark icon (the little book symbol to the left of the Search field; refer to **Figure 13-9**), and then tap the Recent tab to reveal recently visited sites. Tap on a bookmark to go there.

 As you discover later in this chapter in the "Add a Bookmark" task, you can also quickly go to any location you've previously visited and saved using the Bookmarks feature.

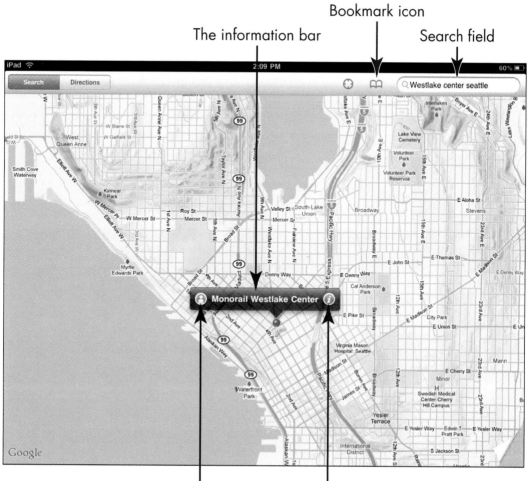

Figure 13-9

 If you enter a destination such as Bronx Zoo, you might want to also enter the city and state. Bronx Zoo landed me in the Woodland Park Zoo in Tacoma for some odd reason!

Drop a Pin

1. Pins are markers; a green pin marks a start location, red pins mark search results, while a blue pin (referred to as the blue marker) marks your iPad's current location.

Display a map that contains a spot where you'd like to drop a pin to help you get directions to or from that site.

2. If you need to, you can zoom in to a more detailed map to get a better view of the location you'd like to pin.

3. Press and hold your finger on the screen at the location where you want to place the pin. The pin appears, together with an information bar (see **Figure 13-10**).

The information bar

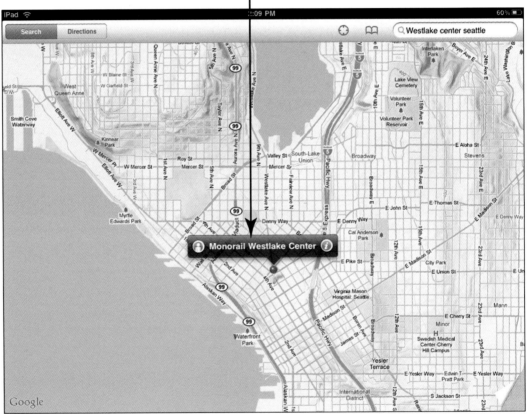

Figure 13-10

4. Tap the Information icon (refer to **Figure 13-10**) on the information bar to display details about the pin location (see **Figure 13-11**).

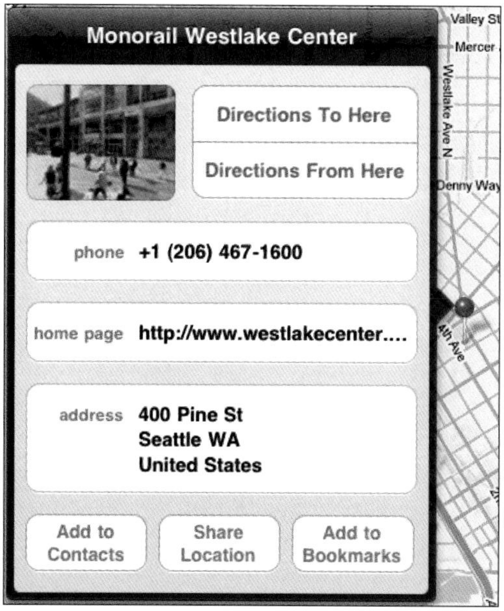

Monorail Westlake Center
Directions To Here
Directions From Here
phone +1 (206) 467-1600
home page http://www.westlakecenter....
address 400 Pine St
Seattle WA
United States
Add to Contacts
Share Location
Add to Bookmarks
Valley St
Mercer
Westlake Ave N
Denny Way
4th Ave

Figure 13-11

To delete a pin you've dropped, tap the pin to display the information bar, and then tap the Information icon. In the information dialog that opens, tap Remove Pin. This only works with pinned sites that aren't bookmarked.

Add and View a Bookmark

1. Bookmarks provide a way to save a destination so you can display a map or directions to it quickly. To add a bookmark to a location, first place a pin on it as described in the preceding task.

2. Tap the Information icon to display the information dialog.

3. Tap the Add to Bookmarks button (see **Figure 13-12**).

4. The Add Bookmark dialog and the keyboard appear (see **Figure 13-13**). If you like, you can modify the name of the bookmark.

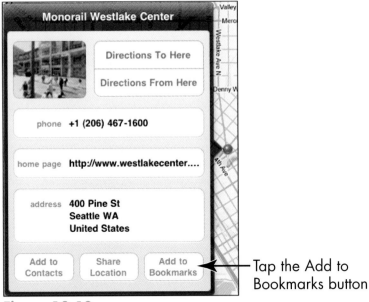

Tap the Add to Bookmarks button

Figure 13-12

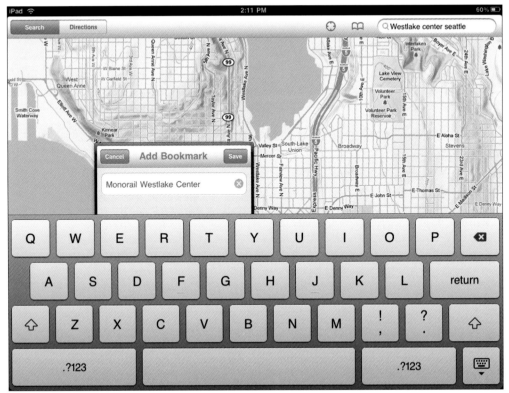

Figure 13-13

5. Tap Save.

6. To view your bookmarks, tap the Bookmarks icon (it looks like a little open book; refer to **Figure** 13-9) at the top of the Maps screen. Be sure the Bookmarks tab is selected; a list of bookmarks is displayed, as shown in **Figure** 13-14.

Figure 13-14

7. Tap on a bookmark to go to the location.

 You can also view recently viewed locations even if you haven't bookmarked them. Tap the Bookmark icon, and then, on the bottom of the Bookmarks dialog that appears, tap Recent. Locations you've visited recently are listed there. Tap on one to return to it.

Delete a Bookmark

1. Tap the Bookmarks icon, and then tap the Bookmarks tab at the bottom of the dialog that appears to be sure you're viewing Bookmarks.

2. Tap the Edit button. A red minus icon appears to the left of your bookmarks, as shown in **Figure 13-15**.

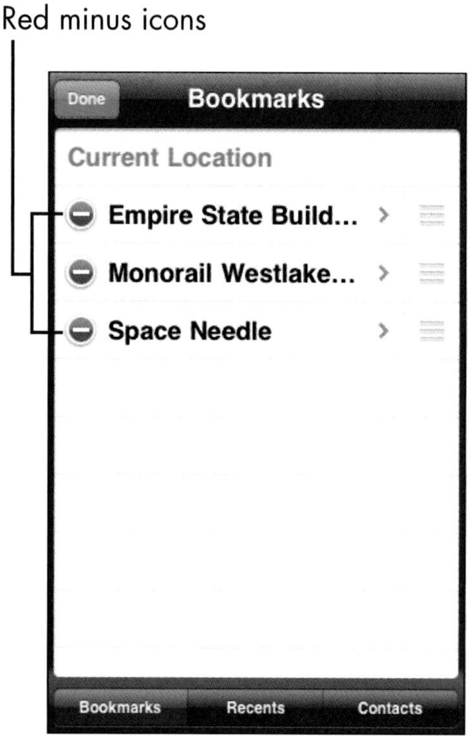

Red minus icons

	Bookmarks
Done	

Current Location

⊖ **Empire State Build...** > ≡

⊖ **Monorail Westlake...** > ≡

⊖ **Space Needle** > ≡

Bookmarks	Recents	Contacts

Figure 13-15

3. Tap a red minus icon.

4. Tap Delete. The bookmark is removed.

 You can also clear out all recent locations stored by Maps to give yourself a clean slate. Tap the Bookmarks icon, and then tap the Recents tab. Tap Clear, and then confirm by tapping Clear All Recents.

Get Directions

1. You can get directions a couple of different ways. With at least one pin on your map in addition to your current location, tap the Directions tab. A line appears, showing the route between your current location and the closest pin (see **Figure 13-16**).

The line indicating your route

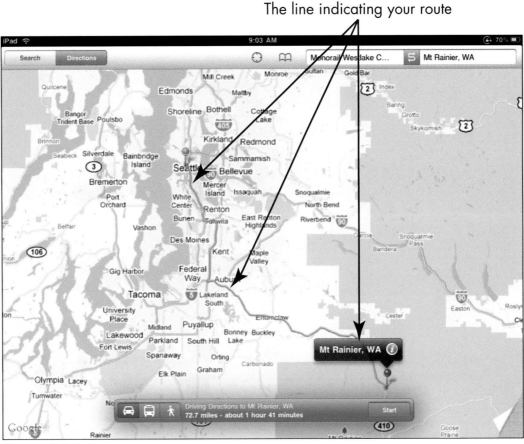

Figure 13-16

2. To show directions from your current location to another pin, tap the other pin and the route is redrawn.

3. You can also enter two locations to get directions from one to the other. With the Directions tab selected in Maps, tap in the field labeled Current Location. The keyboard appears (see **Figure 13-17**).

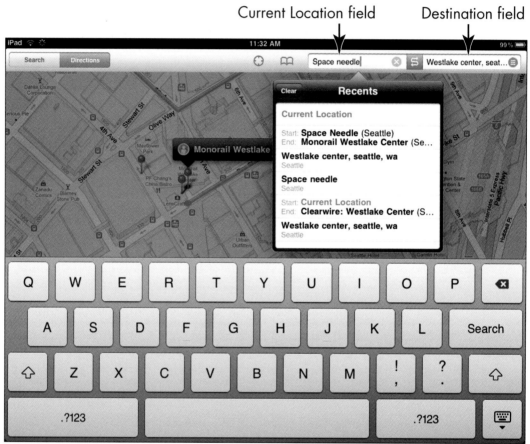

Figure 13-17

4. Enter a different starting location.

5. Tap in the Destination field, enter a destination location, and then press the Search button on the keyboard. The route between the two locations is displayed.

6. You can also tap the Information icon on the information bar that appears above any selected pin and use the

Directions To Here or Directions From Here button to
generate directions (see **Figure 13-18**).

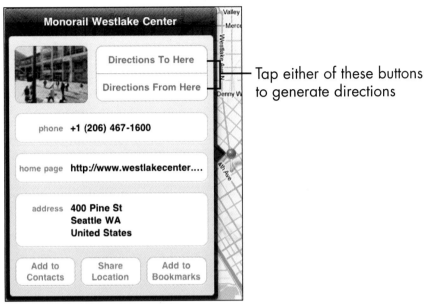

Tap either of these buttons
to generate directions

Figure 13-18

7. With a route displayed, a blue bar appears along the bottom of the Maps screen with information about the distance and time it takes to travel between the two
locations. Here's what you can do with this informa-
tional display:

- Tap the car, bus, or pedestrian logo to get driving,
  public transportation, or walking directions (see
  Figure 13-19).

- Tap Start to change the tools offered: The icon on
  the left showing several lines of text as if in a small
  document takes you to step-by-step directions (see
  Figure 13-20); the arrow keys take you through
  the directions one step at a time.

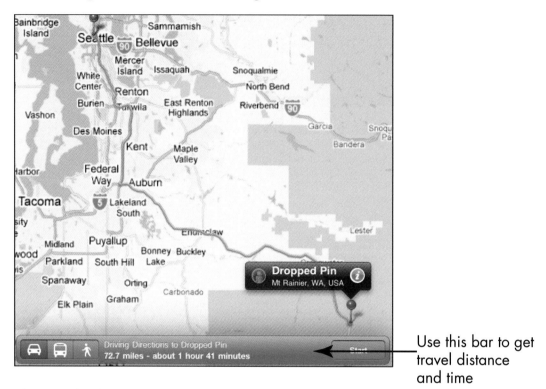

Use this bar to get travel distance and time

Figure 13-19

 In the directions view of Maps, notice the button with a zig-zag line between the Current Location and Destination fields (refer to **Figure 13-17**). After you generate directions from one location to another, tap this button to generate reverse directions. Believe me, they aren't always the same — especially when one-way streets are involved!

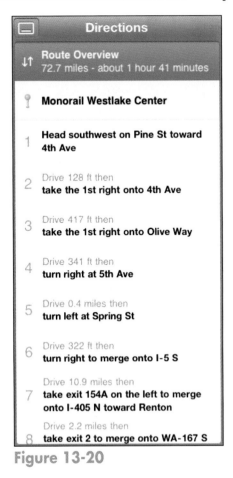

Figure 13-20

Get Information about a Location

1. You've displayed the information dialog for locations to add a bookmark or get directions in previous tasks. Now you focus on the useful information displayed there. Go to a location and tap the pin.

2. In the information bar that appears above the pinned location, tap the Information icon (see **Figure 13-21**).

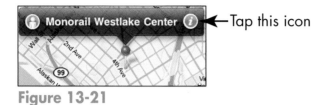

Figure 13-21

3. In the information dialog (see **Figure 13-22**), tap the Web address listed in the Home Page field to be taken to the location's Web page, if it has one associated with it.

Figure 13-22

4. You can also press and hold the Phone or Address fields and use the Copy button to copy the phone number, for example, so you can place it in a Notes document for future reference.

5. Tap outside the information dialog to close it.

Rather than copy and paste information, you can easily save all the information about a location in your Contacts address book. See the "Add a Location to Contacts" task, later in this chapter, to find out how that's done.

View a Location from Street Level

1. You can only view certain locations from street level (see **Figure 13-23**), so you'll have to explore to try this out. In the Search tab of Maps, tap the Search field and enter a location, such as your favorite local shopping mall.

Street view is not available for this location

Figure 13-23

2. When the location appears, tap the Street view icon on its information bar. The Street view appears.

3. When you're in Street view (see **Figure 13-24**), you can tap and drag the screen to look around you in all directions.

4. Tap the small circular map in the bottom-right corner (refer to **Figure 13-24**) to return to the standard map view.

 You can also drag the screen down to get a better look at tall skyscrapers or up to view the street and manhole covers. The small circular map in the bottom-right corner highlights what you're looking at in the specific moment. In addition, street names are displayed down the center of streets.

Tap here to return to the standard map view

Figure 13-24

Use the Compass

1. The Compass feature only works from your current location, so start by tapping the Current Location icon at the top of the Maps screen (refer to **Figure 13-1**).

2. Tap the icon again to turn the Compass on. A small compass appears in the top-right corner of the screen (see **Figure** 13-25).

The Compass

Figure 13-25

3. Move your iPad around in different directions and note that the compass symbol moves as well, indicating which direction you're facing.

4. To turn the Compass off, tap the Current Location icon one more time.

You may get a message that there's interference and the Compass needs resetting. To do so, move away from any electronic equipment that might be causing interference, and move the iPad around in what Apple describes as a figure 8 motion.

 Location Services has to be turned on in iPad Settings for the Compass feature to be available.

Add a Location to Contacts

1. Tap on a pin to display the information bar.

2. Tap on the Information icon.

3. In the information dialog that appears (see **Figure 13-26**), tap Add to Contacts.

Figure 13-26

4. In the following dialog, tap Create New Contact. The New Contact dialog appears (see **Figure** 13-27).

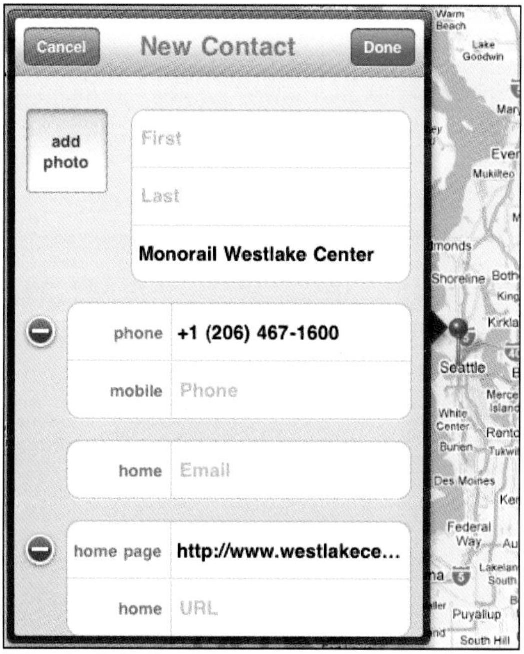

Figure 13-27

5. Whatever information was available about the location has already been entered. Enter any additional information you need, such as name, phone, or e-mail.

6. Tap Done. The information is stored in your Contacts address book.

Share Location Information

1. Tap on a pin to display the information bar.

2. Tap on the Information icon.

3. In the information dialog that appears, tap Share Location.

4. In the e-mail form that appears (see **Figure 13-28**), use the on-screen keyboard to enter a recipient's e-mail address, any Cc/Bcc addresses, and add or change the subject or message as you like.

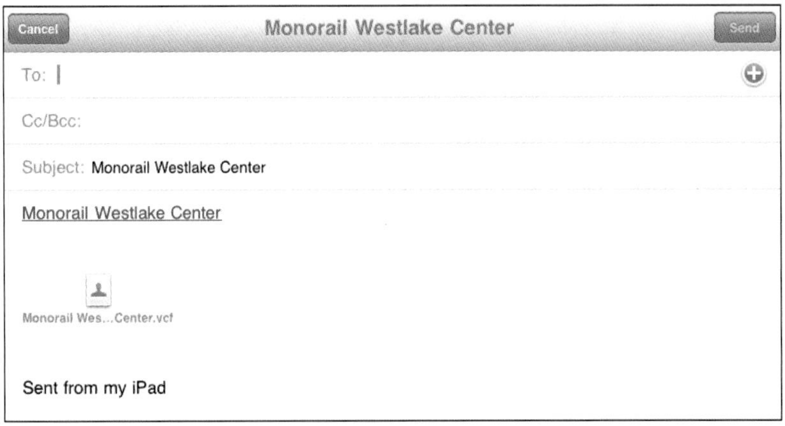

| Cancel | Monorail Westlake Center | Send |

To: |

Cc/Bcc:

Subject: Monorail Westlake Center

Monorail Westlake Center

Monorail Wes...Center.vcf

Sent from my iPad

Figure 13-28

5. Tap Send. A link to the location information in Google Maps is sent to your designated recipient(s).

Part IV
Managing Your Life and Your iPad

The 5th Wave   By Rich Tennant

iPad

"In fact it does come with a compass."

Keeping On Schedule with Calendar

Whether you're retired or still working, you have a busy life full of activities (even busier if you're retired, for some unfathomable reason). You may need a way to keep on top of all those activities and appointments. The Calendar app on your iPad is a simple, elegant, electronic daybook that helps you do just that.

In addition to allowing you to enter events and view them by the day, week, or month, you can set up Calendar to send alerts to remind you of your obligations, and search for events by keywords. You can even set up repeating events, such as your weekly poker game, a get-together with the girls or guys, or a babysitting appointment with your grandchild.

In this chapter, you master the very simple procedures for getting around your calendar, entering and editing events, setting up alerts, and searching.

Get ready to . . .

View Your Calendar

1. Calendar offers several ways to view your schedule. Start by tapping the Calendar app icon on the Home screen to open it.

2. Tap the Day button at the top of the screen to display the Day view (if it's not already displayed). This view, shown in **Figure 14-1,** displays your daily appointments with times listed on the left page, along with a calendar for the month, and an hourly breakdown of the day on the right page. Tap a day on the monthly calendar displayed in the upper-right corner of the left page to change days in this view.

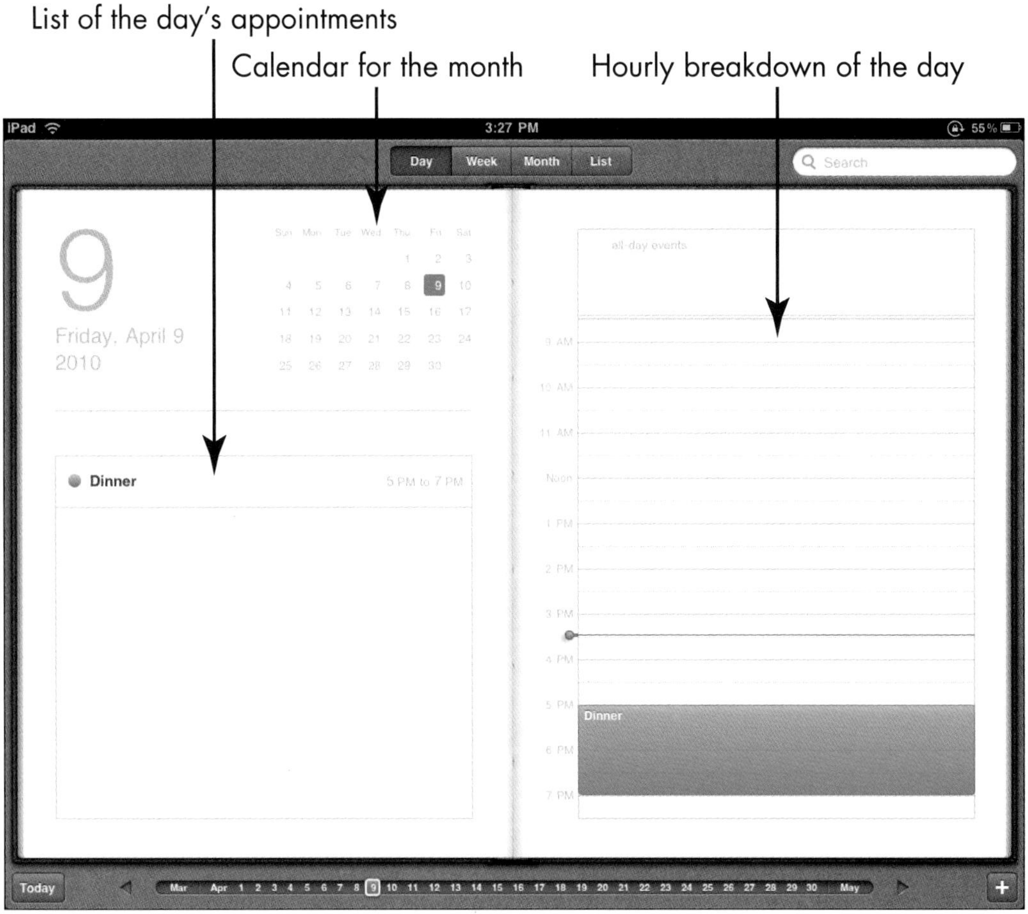

List of the day's appointments

Calendar for the month   Hourly breakdown of the day

Figure 14-1

3. Tap the Week button to view all your events for the current week, as shown in **Figure 14-2**. In this view,
appointments appear with times listed along the left of
the screen.

The Week button

Figure 14-2

4. Tap the Month button to get an overview of your busy
month (see **Figure 14-3**). In this view, you don't see the
timing of each event, but you can spot your busiest days
and what days have room for yet one more event.

5. Finally, tap the List button to see the List view, which displays your daily calendar with a list of all commitments
for the month to the left of it, as shown in **Figure 14-4**.

The Month button

Figure 14-3

6. To move from one day/week/month to another, use the Timeline displayed along the bottom of every view. Tap a day to move to it, or use the Forward or Backward button to move forward or backward one increment at a time: a day at a time in day view, a week at a time in week view, and so on.

7. To jump back to today, tap the Today button in the bottom-left corner of the Calendar.

 For the feel of a real calendar book, rotate your screen when in the Calendar app. It provides a nice book-like experience, especially in the Day view.

Search field

Forward button

Today button

Timeline

Backward button

Add button

Figure 14-4

Add Calendar Events

1. With any view displayed, tap the Add button (the small plus sign in the bottom-right corner of the screen; refer to **Figure** 14-4) to add an event. The Add Event dialog shown in **Figure** 14-5 appears.

2. Enter a title for the event and, if you wish, a location.

3. Tap the Starts/Ends field; the Start & End dialog in **Figure** 14-6 is displayed.

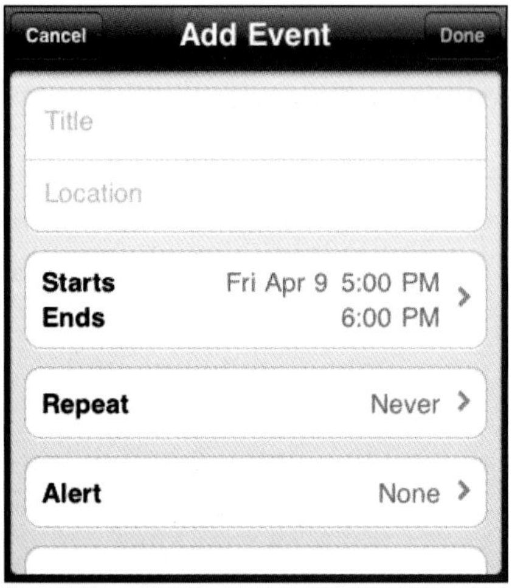

Figure 14-5

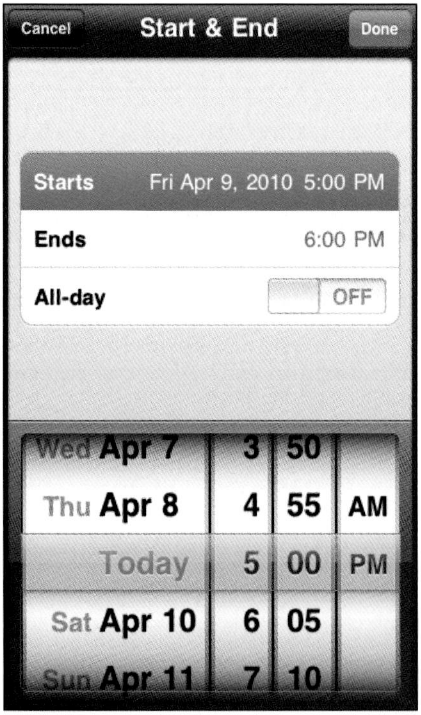

Figure 14-6

4. Place your finger on the date, hour, minute, or AM/PM column and move your finger to scroll up or down. When each item is set correctly, tap Done. (Note that, if the event will last all day, you can simply tap the All-day On/Off button and forget setting start and end times.)

5. If you want to add notes, use your finger to scroll down in the Add Event dialog and tap in the Notes field. Type your note, and then tap the Done button to save the event.

 You can edit any event at any time by simply tapping it in any view of your calendar. The Edit Event dialog appears, offering the same settings as the Add Event dialog shown back in **Figure 14-5**. Tap the Done button to save your changes once you've made them.

Create Repeating Events

1. If you want an event to repeat, as with a weekly or monthly appointment, you can set a repeating event. With any view displayed, tap the Add button to add an event. The Add Event dialog (refer to **Figure 14-5**) appears.

2. Enter a title and location for the event and set the start and end dates/times as shown in the previous task.

3. Tap the Repeat field; the Repeat Event dialog in **Figure 14-7** is displayed.

4. Tap on a preset time interval: Every day, week, 2 weeks, month, or year.

5. Tap Done. You return to the Add Event dialog.

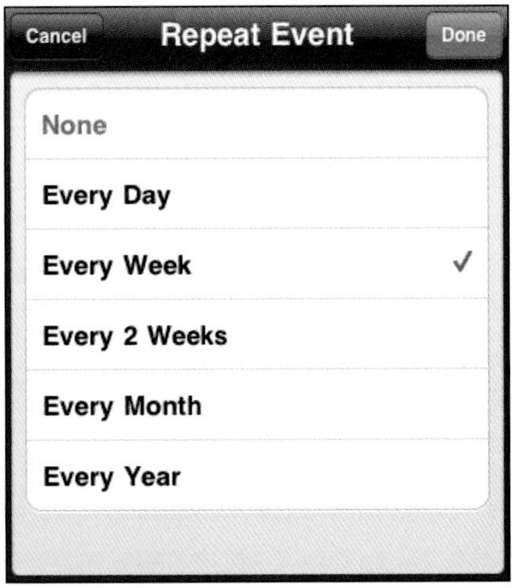

Cancel	**Repeat Event**	Done
None		
Every Day		
Every Week		✓
Every 2 Weeks		
Every Month		
Every Year		

Figure 14-7

6. Tap Done again to save your repeating event.

Some other calendar programs may seem to give you more control over repeating events; for example, they might enable you to make a setting to repeat an event every Tuesday. To do this in iPad's Calendar app, simply add the first event on a Tuesday and make it repeat each week. Easy, huh?

Add Alerts

1. If you want your iPad to alert you when an event is coming up, you can use the Alert feature. First, tap the Settings icon on the Home screen and choose General, and then choose Sounds.

2. If Calendar Alerts is not on, tap the On/Off button to turn it on.

3. Now create an event in your calendar or open an existing one for editing, as covered in the preceding tasks.

4. In the Add Event dialog (refer to **Figure** 14-5), tap the Alert field. The Event Alert dialog appears, as shown in **Figure 14-8**.

Cancel	**Event Alert**	Done
None		
5 minutes before		
15 minutes before	✓	
30 minutes before		
1 hour before		
2 hours before		
1 day before		

Figure 14-8

5. Tap any preset interval, from 5 minutes to 2 days before (remember, you can scroll down in the dialog to see more options).

6. Tap Done to save the alert, and then tap Done in the Add Event dialog to save all settings.

7. Tap the Day button to display the day view of the date of your event; note that the alert and timeframe are listed under the event in that view, as shown in **Figure 14-9**.

 If you work for an organization that uses a Microsoft Exchange account, you can set up your iPad to receive and respond to invitations from others in your company. When somebody sends an invitation that you accept, it appears on your calendar. Check with your company network administrator (who will jump at the chance to get his/her hands on your iPad) or the iPad User Guide to set this up if it sounds useful to you.

An event's alert and timeframe

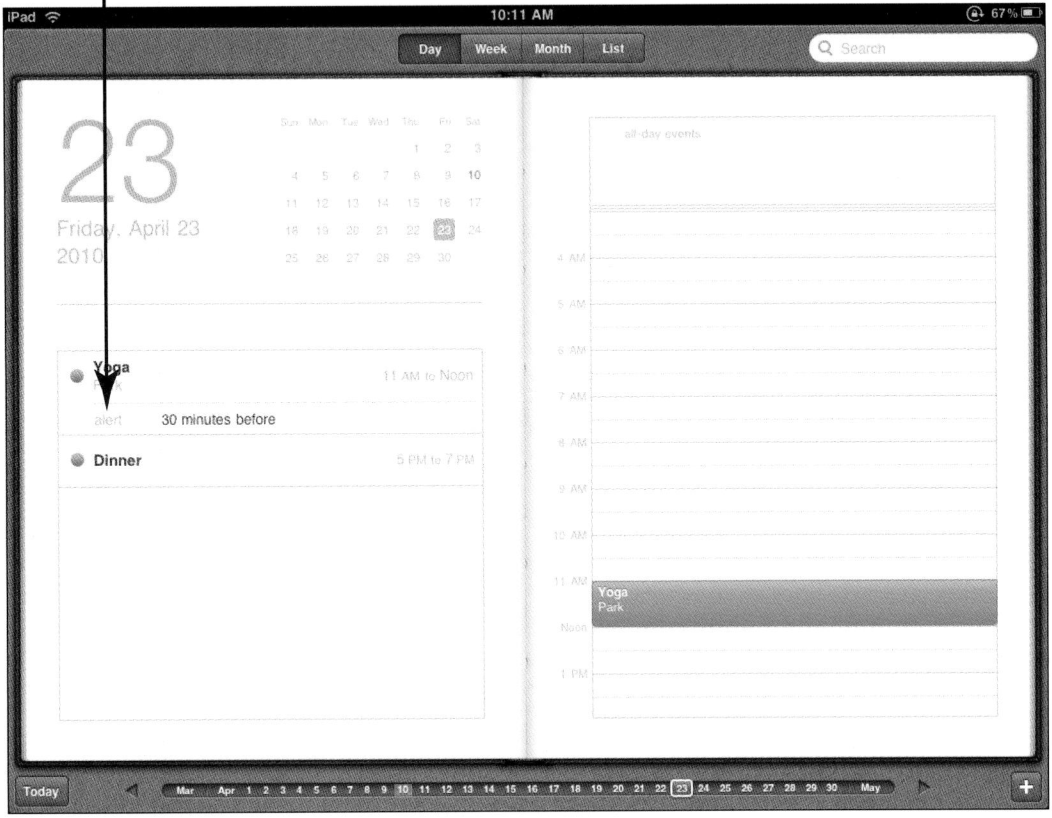

Figure 14-9

Search Calendars

1. With the Calendar open in any view, tap the Search field in the upper-right corner (refer to **Figure** 14-4). The on-screen keyboard appears.

2. Type a word or words to search by and then tap the Search key on the on-screen keyboard. As you type, a Results dialog appears, as shown in **Figure** 14-10.

Figure 14-10

3. Tap on any result to display it in the view you were in when you started the search. A box appears with information about the time of the event and an Edit button you can use to make changes, if you wish, as shown in **Figure** 14-11.

Figure 14-11

Subscribe to and Share Calendars

1. If you use a calendar available through an online service such as Yahoo! or Google, you can subscribe to that calendar to read events saved there on your iPad. Note that you can only read, not edit, such events. Tap the Settings icon on the Home screen to get started.

2. Tap the Mail, Contacts, Calendars option on the left.

3. Tap Add Account. The Add Account options shown in **Figure 14-12** appear.

4. Tap an e-mail choice such as Gmail or Yahoo! Mail.

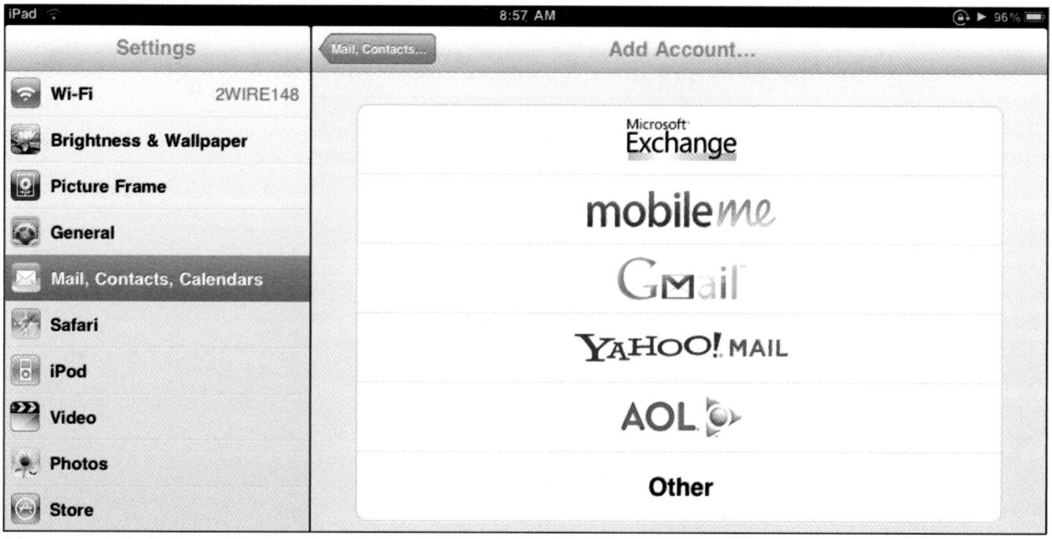

Figure 14-12

5. In the dialog that appears (see **Figure 14-13**), enter your name, e-mail address, and e-mail account password.

Figure 14-13

6. Tap Save. iPad verifies your address.

7. Your iPad retrieves data from your calendar at the interval you have set to fetch data. If you wish to review those settings, tap the Fetch New Data option in the Mail, Contacts, Calendars dialog.

8. In the Fetch New Data dialog that appears (see **Figure 14-14**), be sure that the Push option's On/Off button reads On, and then choose the option you prefer for how frequently data is pushed to your iPad.

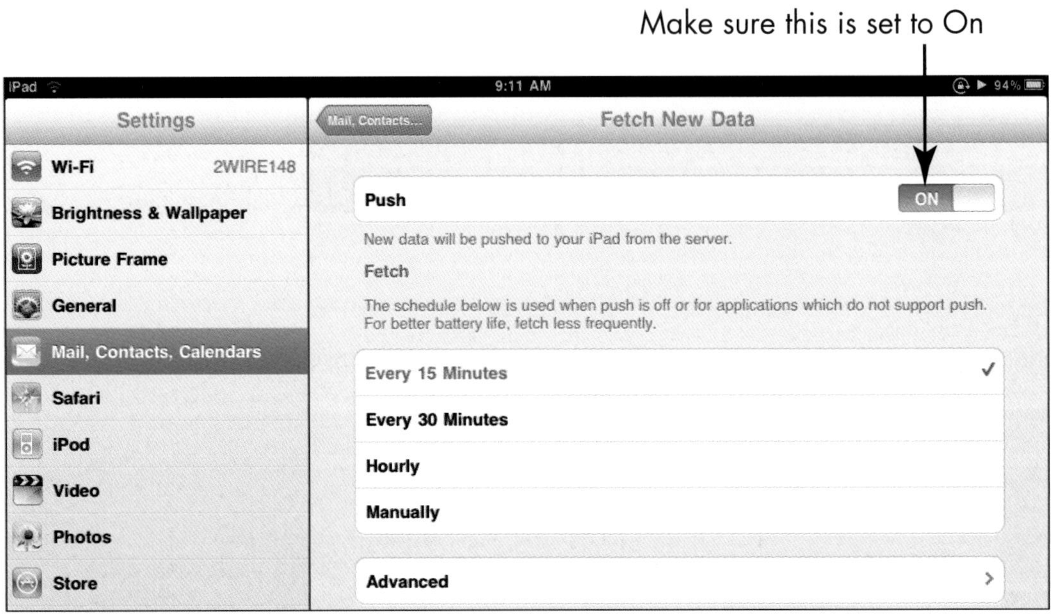

Make sure this is set to On

Figure 14-14

If you use Microsoft Outlook's calendar or iCal on your main computer, you can sync it to your iPad calendar to prevent having to reenter event information. To do this, connect your iPad to your computer with the Dock Connector to USB Cable and use settings in your iTunes account to sync with contacts. Click the Sync button and your calendar settings will be shared between your computer and iPad (in both directions). Learn more about working with iTunes to manage your iPad content in Chapter 3.

You can also have calendar events sent if you subscribe to a push service such as MobileMe. If you choose to have data pushed to your iPad more frequently, it may cause your battery to drain a bit faster.

Delete Events

1. When that luncheon or meeting is cancelled, it is a good idea to delete the old appointment. With Calendar open, tap an event. Then tap the Edit button in the information bar that appears (see **Figure 14-15**).

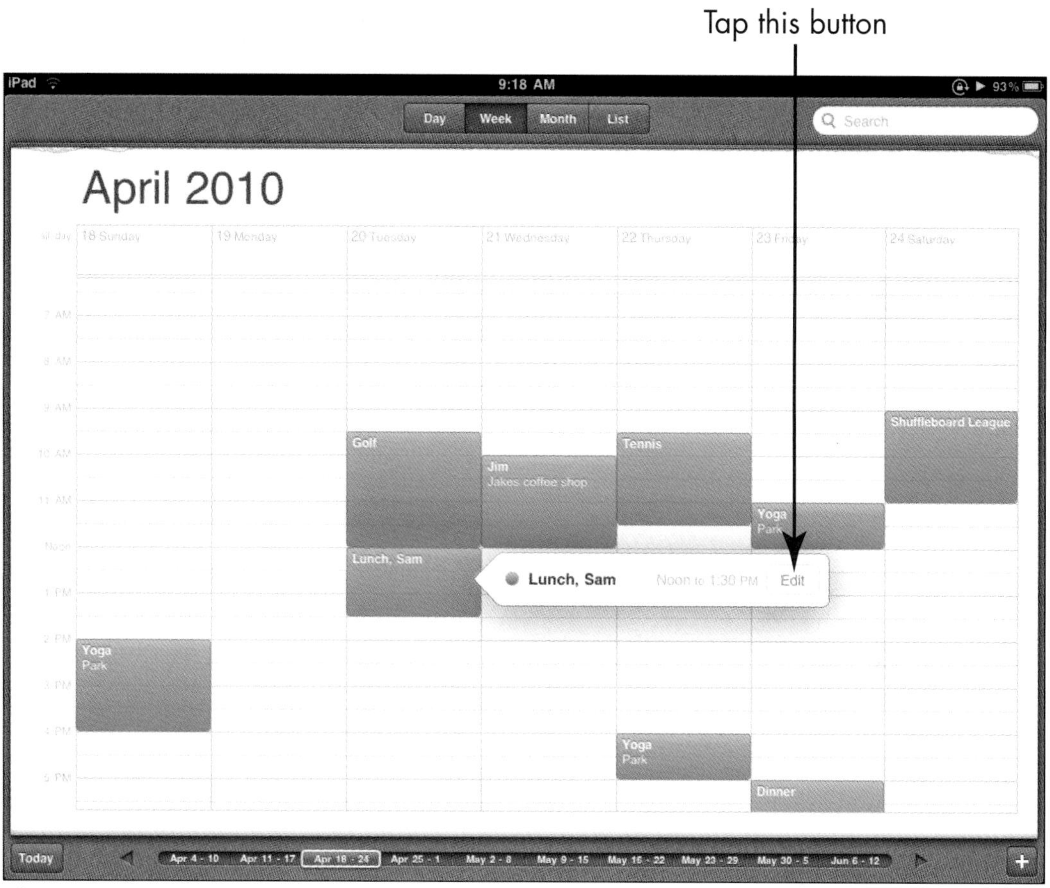

Tap this button

Figure 14-15

2. In the Edit Event dialog, tap the Delete Event button (see **Figure 14-16**).

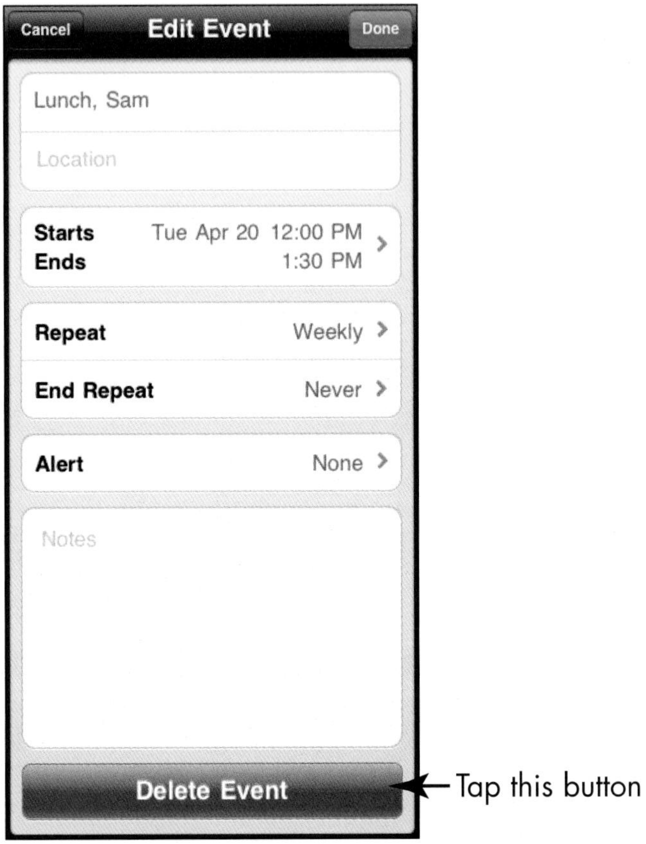

Cancel	Edit Event	Done

Lunch, Sam

Location

| **Starts** | Tue Apr 20 12:00 PM | > |
| **Ends** | 1:30 PM | |

| **Repeat** | Weekly > |

| **End Repeat** | Never > |

| **Alert** | None > |

Notes

Delete Event ←— Tap this button

Figure 14-16

3. Confirming options appear; if this is a repeating event, you have the option of deleting this instance of the event or this and all future instances of the event (see **Figure 14-17**). Tap the button for the option you prefer. The event is deleted and you're returned to the Calendar view.

 If an event is moved but not cancelled, you don't have to delete the exiting one and create a new one; simply edit the event to change the day and time in the Event dialog.

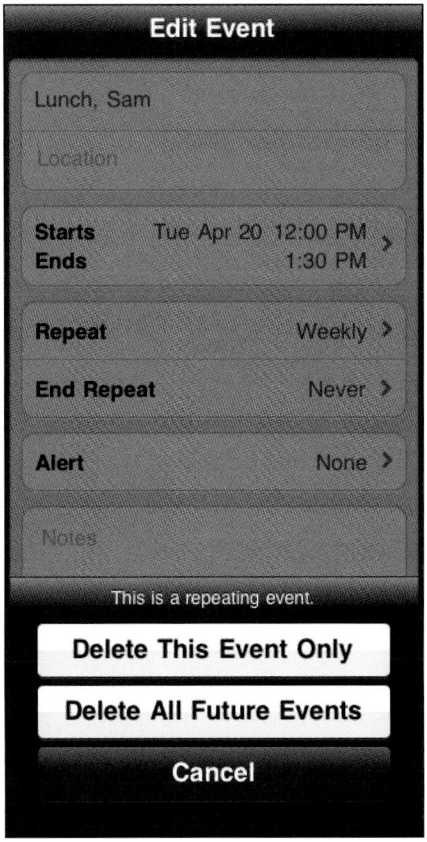

Edit Event

Lunch, Sam

Location

Starts	Tue Apr 20 12:00 PM	>
Ends	1:30 PM	

Repeat   Weekly >

End Repeat   Never >

Alert   None >

Notes

This is a repeating event.

Delete This Event Only

Delete All Future Events

Cancel

Figure 14-17

Managing Contacts

Contacts is the iPad equivalent of that dog-eared address book that sits by your phone. The Contacts application is simple to set up and use, and it has some powerful little features beyond simply storing names, addresses, and phone numbers.

For example, you can pinpoint a contact's address in iPad's Maps application. You can use your contacts to address e-mails quickly. If you store contact records that include a Web site, you can use a link in Contacts to view that Web site instantly. And, of course, you can easily search for a contact.

In this chapter, you discover the various features of Contacts, including how to save yourself time entering their information by syncing a Google or Yahoo! contacts list to your iPad.

Add Contacts

1. Tap the Contacts app icon on the Home screen to open the application. If you haven't entered any contacts yet, you see a blank address book like the one shown in **Figure 15-1**.

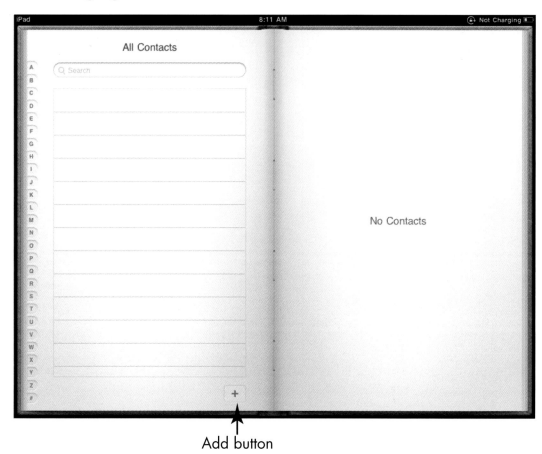

Add button

Figure 15-1

2. Tap the Add button (the button with a small plus sign on it). A New Contact page opens and the on-screen keyboard is displayed, as you can see in **Figure 15-2**.

3. Enter any contact information that you wish (only a first name in the First field is required).

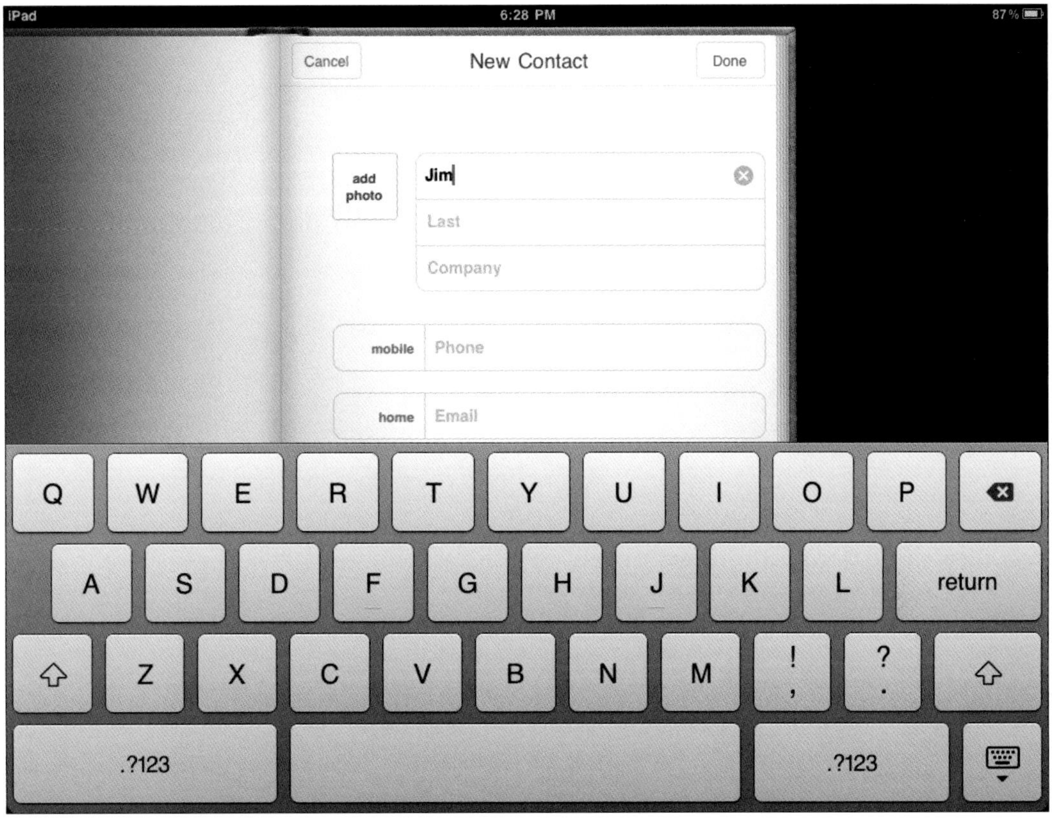

Figure 15-2

4. To scroll down the contact page and see more fields, flick up on the page with your finger.

5. If you want to add a mailing or street address you can tap Add New Address, which opens up additional entry fields.

6. To add an additional information field, tap Add Field. In the Add Field dialog that appears (see **Figure 15-3**), choose a field to add (you may have to flick the page up with your finger to view all the fields).

Figure 15-3

7. Tap the Done button when you finish making entries. The new contact appears in your address book. (**Figure 15-4** shows an address book with several entries added.)

 If your contact has a name that's difficult for you to pronounce, consider adding the Phonetic First Name or Phonetic Last Name fields to that person's record (refer to Step 6).

Sync Contacts Using iTunes

1. You can use your iTunes account accessed from your computer to sync contacts between your Yahoo! or Gmail e-mail account (such as the one shown in **Figure 15-5**), for example, and your iPad Contacts application. This sync works in both directions: Contacts from iPad are sent to your e-mail account and contacts from your e-mail account are sent to iPad. First, connect your iPad to your computer with the Dock Connector to USB Cable.

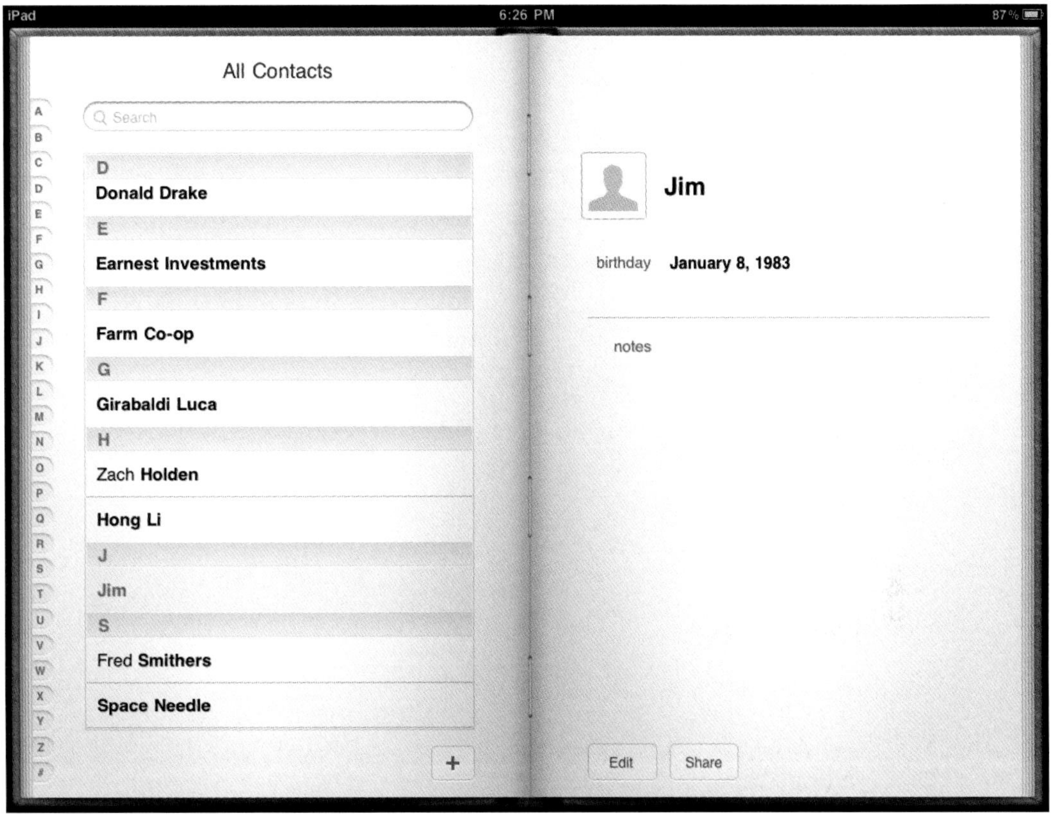

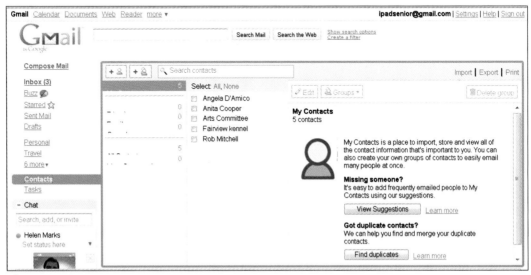

Figure 15-4

Figure 15-5

2. In the iTunes site that opens on your computer, double-click the name of your iPad (such as Earl's iPad), which is now listed in the left navigation area of iTunes.

3. Click on the Info tab, shown in **Figure 15-6**.

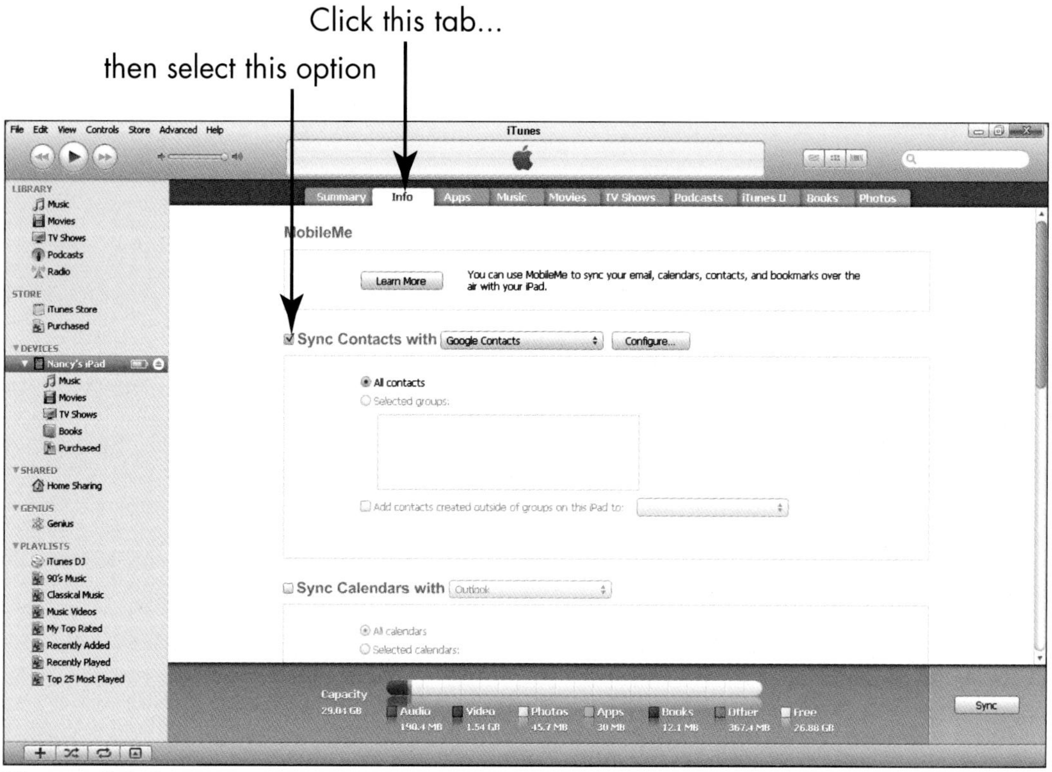

Click this tab...

then select this option

Figure 15-6

4. Click to select the Sync Contacts check box, and then choose your e-mail provider from the drop-down list (Windows) or pop-up menu (Mac).

5. Click the Apply button in the lower-right corner. After the change is applied, this button turns into the Sync button.

6. Click the Sync button and your iPad screen changes to show that syncing is in progress.

7. When the sync is complete, open Contacts on your iPad. All contacts have been brought over to it.

8. Unplug the Dock Connector to USB Cable.

 You can also use a MobileMe or Microsoft Exchange account to sync contacts with iPad, but MobileMe charges a subscription fee. Microsoft Exchange may, for example, be what a company uses for its networked e-mail accounts, so if you're retired this may not be an option.

Assign a Photo to a Contact

1. With Contacts open, tap on the contact to whose record you want to add a photo.

2. Tap the Edit button.

3. In the Info page that appears (see **Figure 15-7**), tap Add Photo.

4. In the Photo Albums dialog that appears (refer to **Figure 15-7**), tap either Saved Photos or Photo Library, depending on where the photo is stored. Saved photos are ones you've downloaded to your iPad or taken using the screen capture feature; the Photo Library contains photos synced from your computer.

Tap here...then tap on the photo's location

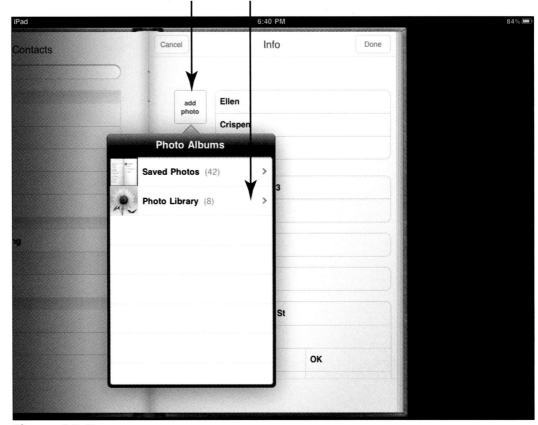

Figure 15-7

5. In the photo album that appears, tap on a photo to select it. The Choose Photo dialog shown in **Figure 15-8** appears.

6. Tap the Use button to use the photo for this contact. The photo appears in the contact Info page (see **Figure 15-9**).

7. Tap Done to save changes to the contact.

Figure 15-8

Figure 15-9

While in the Choose Photo dialog in Step 5, you can modify the photo before saving it to the contact information. You can pinch to expand the photo and move it around the space to focus on a particular section and then tap the Use button to use the modified version.

Search Contacts

1. With Contacts open, tap in the Search field at the top of the left-hand page (see **Figure 15-10**). The on-screen keyboard opens.

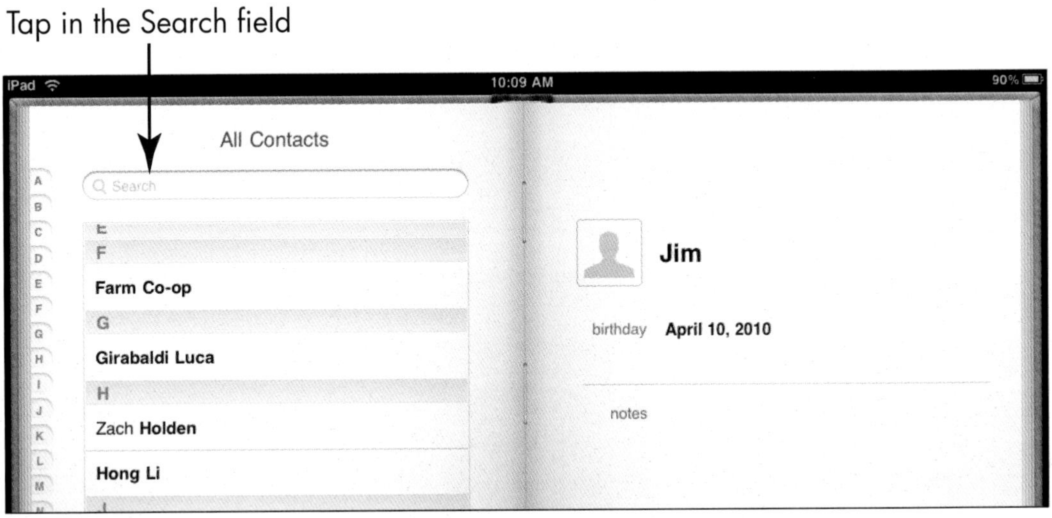

Tap in the Search field

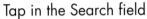

All Contacts

Q Search

E
F
Farm Co-op
G
Girabaldi Luca
H
Zach Holden
Hong Li

Jim

birthday   **April 10, 2010**

notes

Figure 15-10

2. Type the first letter of either the first or last name; all matching results will appear, as shown in **Figure 15-11**. In the example, typing "N" displays Nancy Boysen, Nellie Dillon, and the Space Needle in the results, which all have an "N" starting their first or last name.

3. Tap a contact in the results to display their information on the right page (refer to **Figure 15-11**).

 You can't search by phone number, Web site, or address in Contacts at the time of this writing. We can only hope that Apple will add that functionality in future versions of the app!

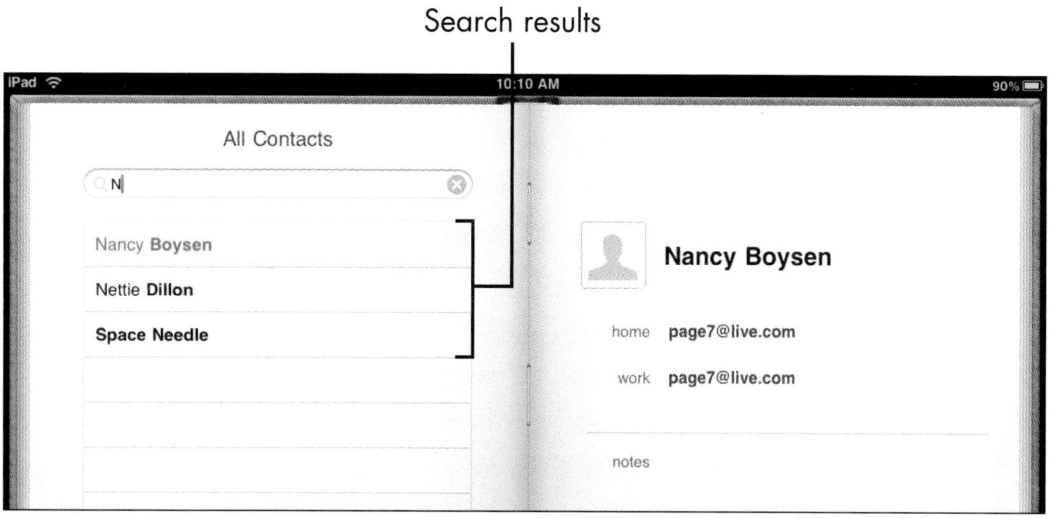

Search results

All Contacts

Nancy **Boysen**

Nettie **Dillon**

Space Needle

Nancy Boysen

home **page7@live.com**

work **page7@live.com**

notes

Figure 15-11

 You can also use the alphabetical listing to locate a contact. Tap and drag to scroll down the list of contacts on the All Contacts page on the left. You can also tap on any of the tabbed letters along the left side of the page to quickly scroll to the entries that start with that letter.

Go to a Contact's Web Site

1. If you entered information in the Home Page field for a contact, it automatically becomes a link in the contact's record. Tap the Contacts app icon on the Home screen to open Contacts.

2. Tap on a contact to display their contact information on the right-hand page, and then tap the link in the Home Page field (see **Figure 15-12**).

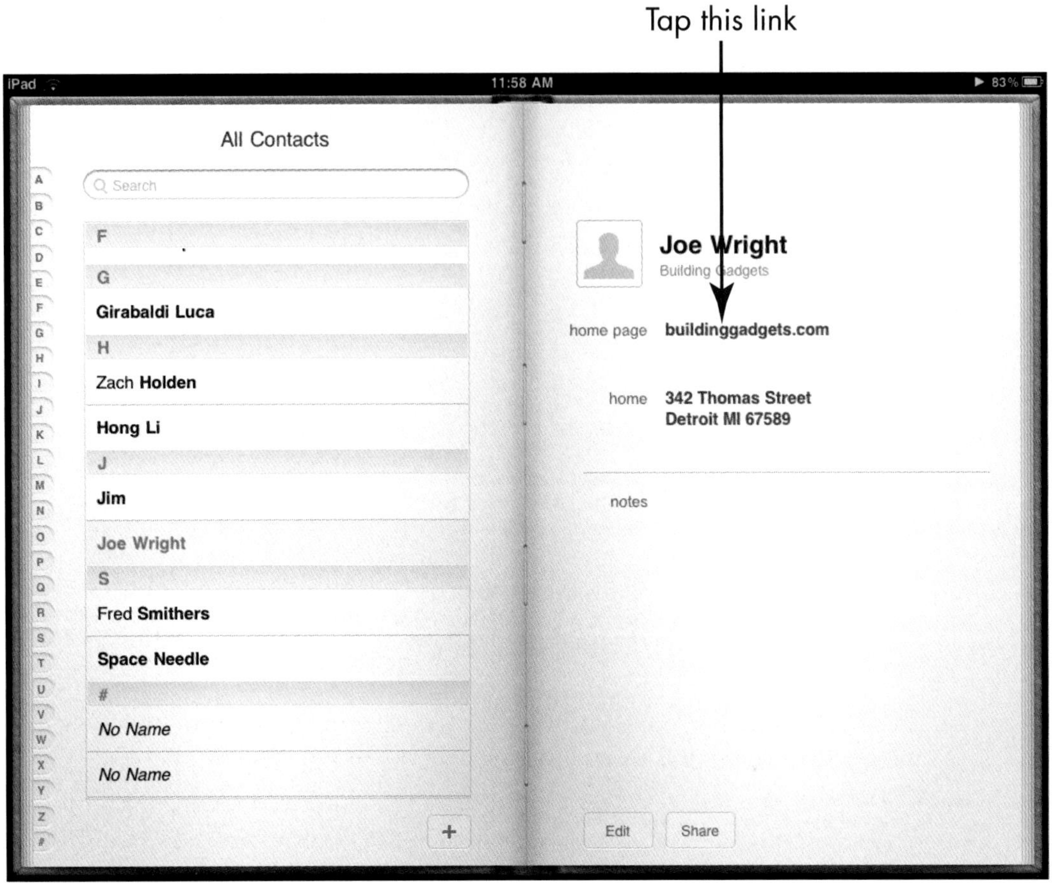

Tap this link
iPad
11:58 AM
83%
All Contacts
Search
F
G
Girabaldi Luca
H
Zach Holden
Hong Li
J
Jim
Joe Wright
S
Fred Smithers
Space Needle
#
No Name
No Name
Joe Wright
Building Gadgets
home page
buildinggadgets.com
home
342 Thomas Street
Detroit MI 67589
notes
Edit
Share

Figure 15-12

3. The Safari browser opens with the Web page displayed (see **Figure 15-13**).

There is no way to go directly back to Contacts after you follow a link to a Web site. You have to tap the Home button, and then tap the Contacts app icon again to reenter the application.

Figure 15-13

Address E-Mails Using Contacts

1. If you entered an e-mail address for a contact, it automatically becomes a link in the contact's record. Tap the Contacts app icon on the Home screen to open Contacts.

2. Tap on a contact to display their contact information on the right-hand page, and then tap on their e-mail address link (see **Figure 15-14**).

3. A New Message dialog appears, as shown in **Figure 15-15**.

4. Use the on-screen keyboard to enter a subject and message.

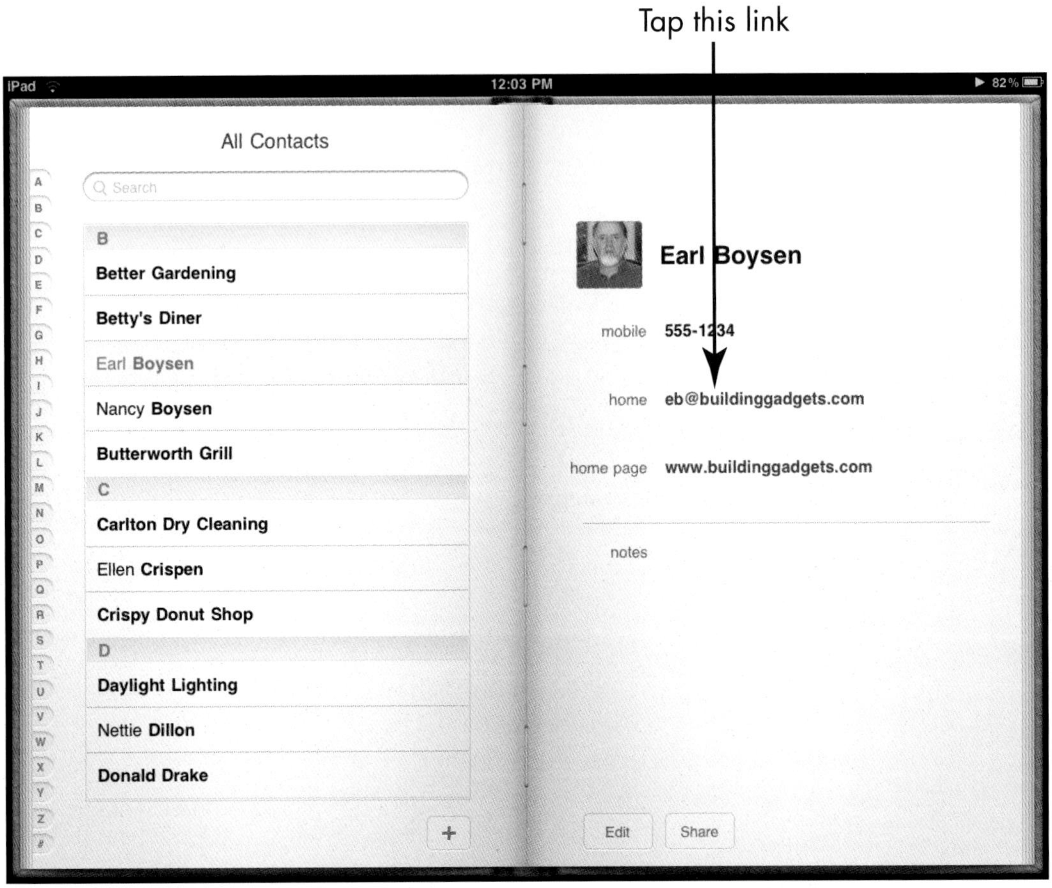

Figure 15-14

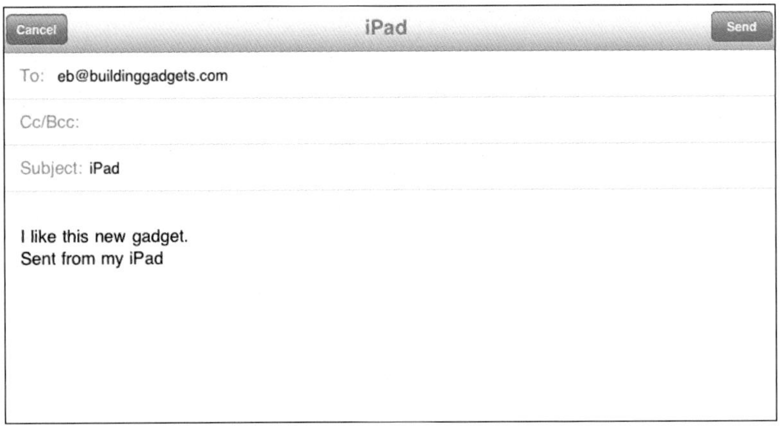

Figure 15-15

5. Tap the Send button. The message goes on its way!

Share Contacts

1. After you've entered contact information, you can share it with others via an e-mail message. With Contacts open, tap a contact name to display its information.

2. On the information page, tap the Share button (see **Figure 15-16**). A New Message form appears.

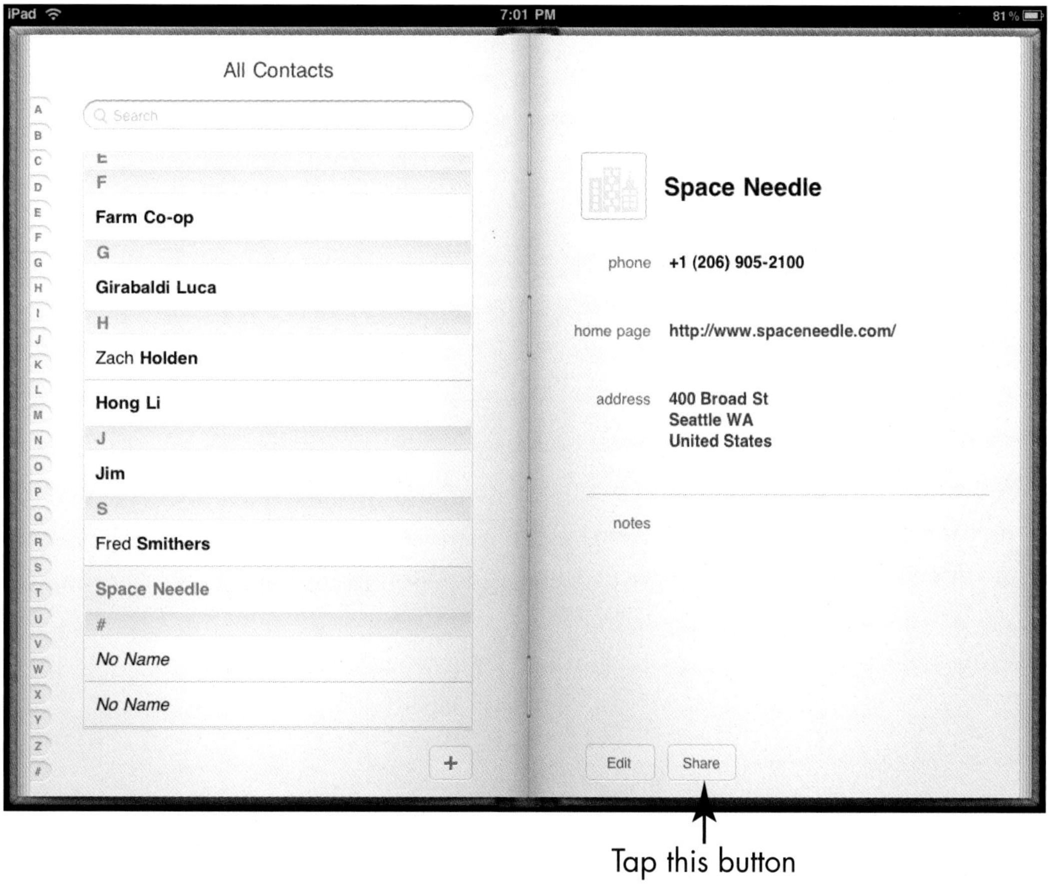

Tap this button

Figure 15-16

3. In the New Message form shown in **Figure 15-17,** use the on-screen keyboard to enter the recipient's e-mail address.

Cancel	New Message	Send

To: eb@buildinggadgets.com

Cc/Bcc:

Subject: |

Space Needle.vcf

Sent from my iPad

Figure 15-17

4. Enter information in the Subject field.

5. If you like, enter a message, and then tap the Send button. The message goes to your recipient with the contact information attached as a `.vcf` file (the vCard format which is commonly used to transmit contact information).

 When somebody receives a vCard containing contact information, he or she need only click on the attached file to open it. At that point, depending on their e-mail or contact management program, they can perform various actions to save the content. Other iPhone or iPad users can easily import `.vcf` records into their own Contacts apps.

View a Contact's Location in Maps

1. If you've entered a person's address in Contacts, you have a shortcut for viewing that person's location in the Maps application. Tap the Contacts app icon on the Home screen to open it.

2. Tap the contact you want to view to display his or her information.

3. Tap the address. Maps opens and displays a map to that address (see **Figure 15-18**).

Figure 15-18

 This works with more than your friends' addresses. You can save information for your favorite restaurant, movie theater, or any place else and use Contacts to jump to the associated Web site in the Safari browser or address in Maps. For more about using Safari see Chapter 5. For more about the Maps application, see Chapter 13.

Delete Contacts

1. When it's time to remove a name or two from your Contacts, it's easy to do. With Contacts open, tap the contact you want to delete.

2. On the information page on the right, tap the Edit button at the bottom of the page.

3. On the Info page that displays, drag your finger upward to scroll down and then tap the Delete Contact button (see **Figure 15-19**).

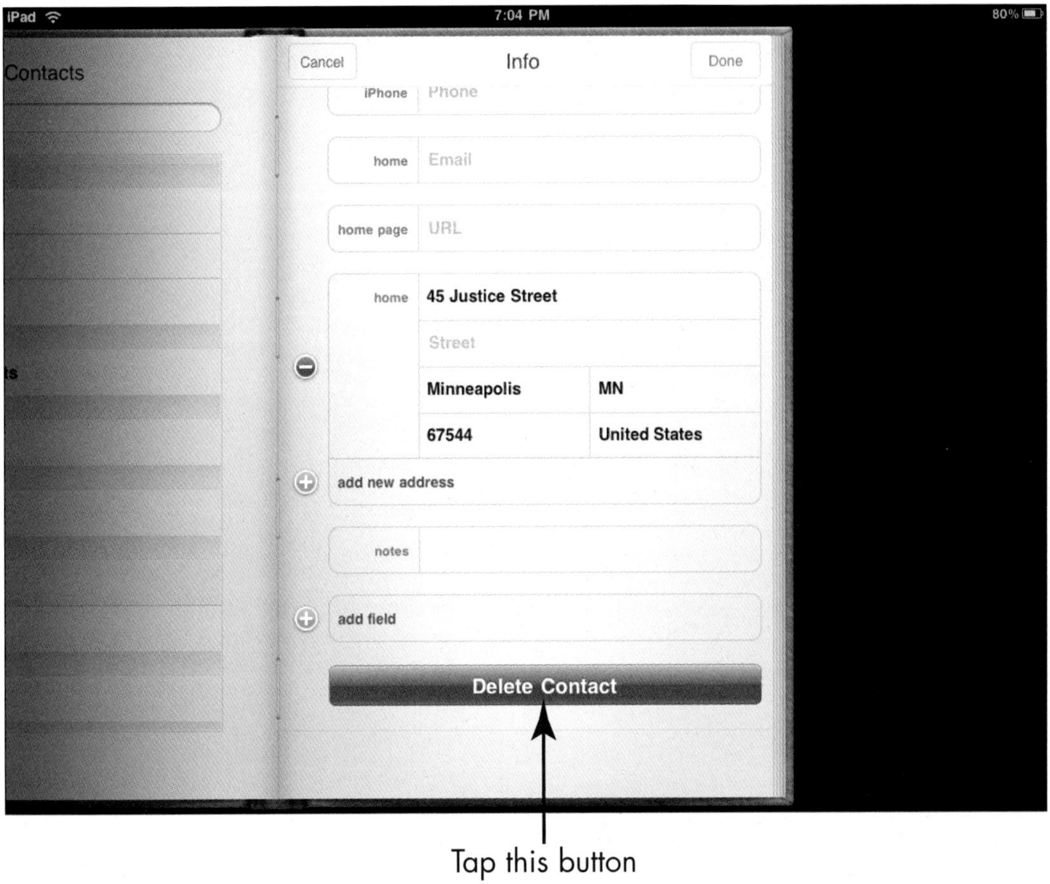

Tap this button

Figure 15-19

4. The confirming dialog shown in **Figure 15-20** appears; tap the Delete button to confirm deletion.

Delete Contact

Delete Cancel ◄── Tap this button

Figure 15-20

 During this process, if you change your mind before you tap Delete, tap the Cancel button in Step 4. But be careful: once you tap Delete, there's no going back!

Making Notes

Chapter 16

*N*otes is a built-in application that you can use to do everything from jotting down notes at meetings to keeping to-do lists. It isn't a robust word processor like Apple's Pages or Microsoft's Word by any means, but for taking notes on- the-fly or writing a few pages of your novel-in-progress while you sit and sip a cup of tea on your deck, it's a great option.

In this chapter, you discover how to enter and edit text in Notes, and manage notes by navigating among them, searching for content, e-mailing them, or deleting a note.

Open a Blank Note

1. To get started with Notes, tap the Notes app icon on the Home screen. If you've never used Notes, it opens with a new, blank note displayed. (If you have used Notes before, it opens to the last note you were working on. If that's the case, you might want to jump to the next task to create a new blank note). Depending on how you have your iPad oriented, you see the view in **Figure 16-1** (portrait) or **Figure 16-2** (landscape).

Figure 16-1

2. Tap the blank page. The on-screen keyboard shown in **Figure 16-3** appears.

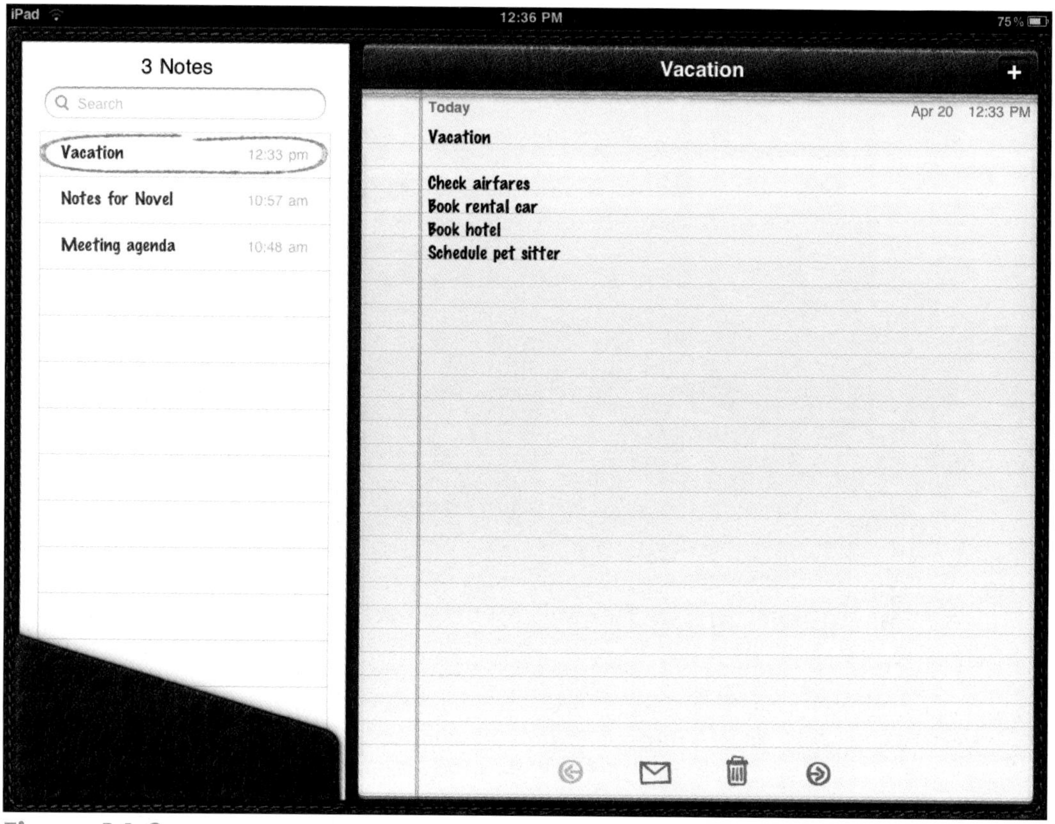

Figure 16-2

Figure 16-3

3. Tap keys on the keyboard to enter text. If you want to enter numbers or symbols, tap either of the keys labeled .?123 on the keyboard. The numbers keyboard shown in **Figure 16-4** appears. When you want to return to the regular keyboard, tap either of the keys labeled ABC.

Figure 16-4

4. To capitalize a letter, tap the Shift key at the same time that you tap the letter.

5. When you want to start a new paragraph or the next item in a list, tap the Return key.

6. To edit text, tap the text you want to edit and use the Delete key to delete text to the left of the cursor, or type new text.

 When you have the numbers keyboard displayed (refer to **Figure 16-4**), you can tap either of the keys labeled #+= to access more symbols, such as the percentage sign, the symbol for euros, and additional bracket styles. With some of these keys, pressing and holding them displays alternate characters.

 No need to save a note — it's automatically kept until you delete it.

Create a New Note

 1. With one note open, to create a new note, tap the New Note button (the one with the + symbol on it) in the top-right corner.

2. A new, blank note appears (refer to **Figure 16-1**). Enter and edit text as described in the previous task.

If you're in portrait orientation and want to see the list of saved notes beside the current note, switch to landscape orientation on your iPad.

Use Copy and Paste

1. The Notes app includes essential editing tools you're probably familiar with from other word processors: copy and paste. With a note displayed, press and hold your finger on a word. The toolbar shown in **Figure 16-5** appears.

iPad	1:32 PM	70%
Notes	**Meeting agenda**	+

Today   Apr 20   10:48 AM

Meeting agenda

| Select | Select All | Paste | port
2. Dis... .. ...w....s ...g..
3. Appoint new secretary
4.

Press and hold on a word to display this toolbar

Figure 16-5

2. Tap the Select button. The toolbar shown in **Figure 16-6** appears.

iPad	2:24 PM	62%
Notes	**Notes for Novel**	+

Today   Apr 20   2:20 PM

Notes for Novel

Mary is a nurse at an inner city ho... . She stumbles upon a plot by the hospital board to cover up treatment errors in the c... Copy ...

John is a famous surgeon who also suspects a colleague of negligent practices.

Tap this button

Figure 16-6

3. Tap the Copy button.

4. Press and hold your finger in the document where you want to place the copied text.

5. In the toolbar that appears (see **Figure 16-7**), tap the Paste button. The copied text appears.

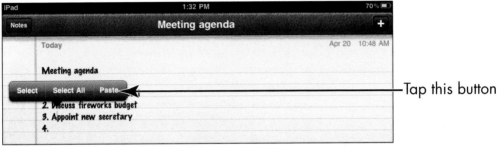

Tap this button

Figure 16-7

 If you want to select all the text in a note to either delete or copy it, tap the Select All button in the toolbar shown in **Figure 16-5**. A Cut/Copy/Paste toolbar appears that you can use to deal with the selected text.

 To delete text, you can use the Select or Select All command, and then press the Delete key on the on-screen keyboard.

Display the Notes List

1. Tap the Notes app icon on the Home screen to open it.

2. If you're using landscape orientation, a list of notes appears by default on the left side of the screen (refer to **Figure 16-2**). If you're using portrait orientation, you can display this list by tapping the Notes button in the top-left corner of the screen; the notes list appears, as shown in **Figure 16-8**.

iPad	1:41 PM	68%
Notes	Meeting agenda	+

————————————Tap this button...

| 3 Notes | Apr 20   1:38 PM |

————————————to display the list
of notes

Q Search

Meeting agenda	1:38 pm
Vacation	12:33 pm
Notes for Novel	10:57 am

Figure 16-8

3. Tap any note on the list to display it.

 Notes names your note using the first line of text. If you want to rename a note, display that note, tap at the end of the first line of text, and tap the Backspace key on your keyboard. Enter a new title; it's reflected as the name of your note in the notes list.

Move among Notes

1. You have a couple of ways to move among notes that you've created. Tap the Notes app icon on the Home screen to open it.

2. With the notes list displayed (you can do this by either turning iPad to a landscape orientation or tapping the Notes button in portrait orientation; see the previous task for more on viewing the notes list), tap a note to open it.

3. Tap the Next or Previous button (the right- and left-facing arrows on the bottom of the Notes pad shown in **Figure 16-9**) to move among notes.

Tap either of
these buttons

Figure 16-9

Notes enables you to enter multiple notes with the
same title, which causes confusion. Instead, name
your notes uniquely!

Search Notes

1. You can search to locate a note that contains certain text.
The Search feature only lists notes that contain your
search criteria; it doesn't actually highlight and show you
every instance of the word or words that you enter. Tap
the Notes app icon on the Home screen to open it.

2. Either hold the iPad in landscape orientation or tap the
Notes button in the portrait orientation to display the
notes list shown in **Figure 16-10.**

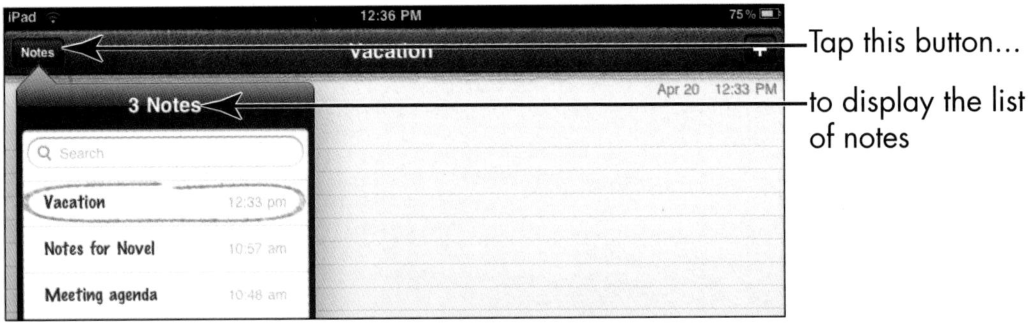

Tap this button...

to display the list
of notes

Figure 16-10

3. Tap in the Search field at the top of the notes list. The
on-screen keyboard appears, as shown in **Figure 16-11.**

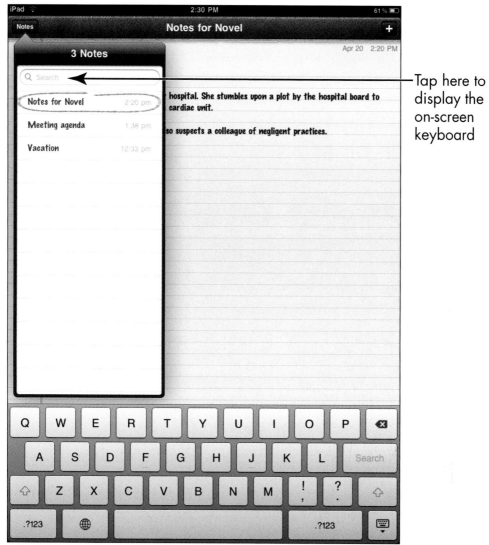

Tap here to
display the
on-screen
keyboard

Figure 16-11

4. Begin to enter the search term. All notes that contain
matching words appear on the list, as shown in **Figure
16-12.**

iPad	1:52 PM	66%
Notes	**Meeting agenda**	+
2 Notes		Apr 20 1:38 PM
Q Re	⊗	
Meeting agenda	1:38 pm	
Vacation	12:33 pm	

Figure 16-12

5. Tap a note to display it and then locate the instance of the matching word the old-fashioned way — by scanning through it.

 If you want to look for a note based on how long ago you created it, it might help you to know that notes are stored with the most recently created or modified notes at the top of the notes list. Older notes fall toward the bottom of the list. The day you last modified each note is also listed in the notes list to help you out.

E-Mail a Note

1. If you want to share what you wrote with a friend or colleague, you can easily e-mail the contents of a note. With a note displayed, tap the E-Mail button on the bottom of the screen, as shown in **Figure 16-13.**

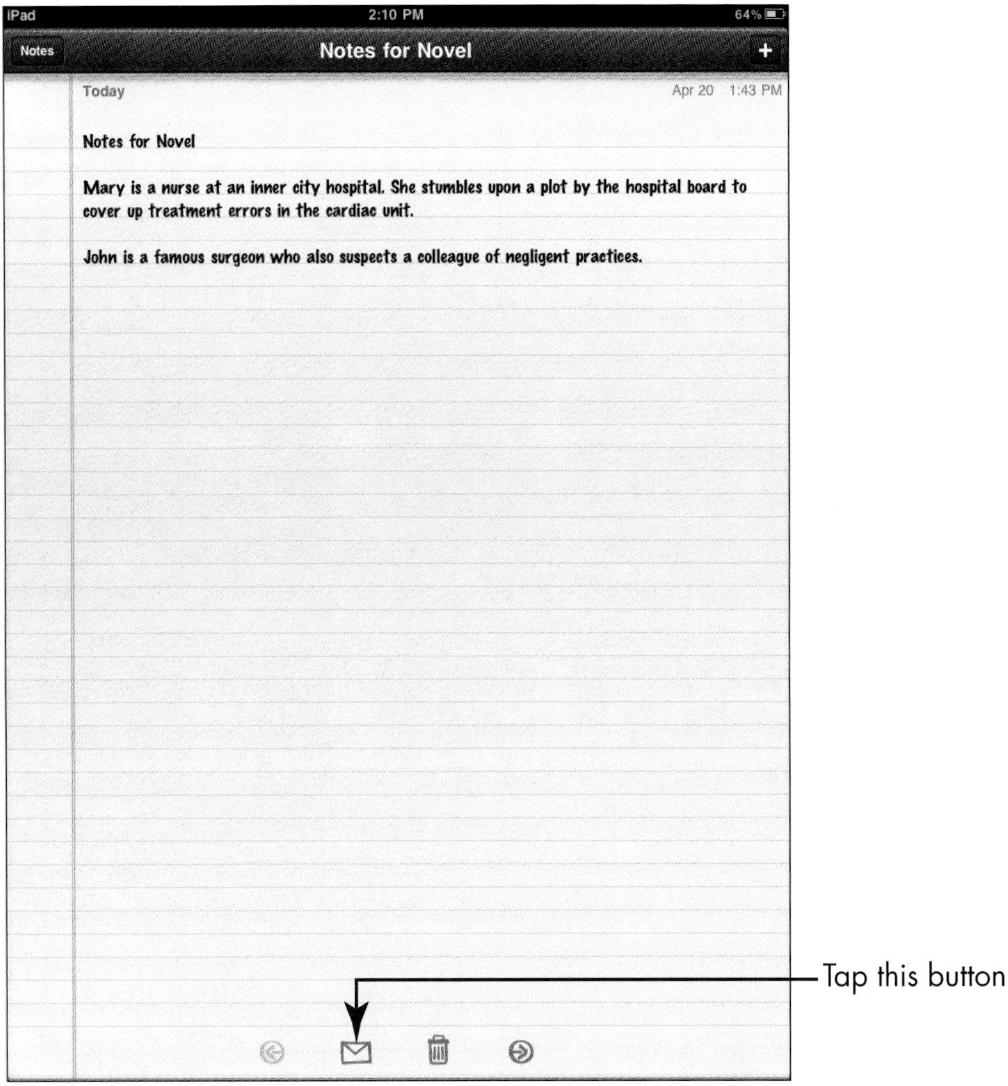

Tap this button

Figure 16-13

2. In the e-mail form that appears (see **Figure 16-14**), type one or more e-mail addresses in the appropriate fields. At least one e-mail address must appear in the To field.

iPad	2:03 PM	65% 🔋
Cancel	Meeting agenda	Send

To: ipadsenior@gmail.com   ⊕   ——— Enter e-mail

Cc/Bcc: addresses here

Subject: Meeting agenda

Meeting agenda

1. Review committee report
2. Discuss fireworks budget
3. Appoint new secretary
4. Appoint new member-at-large

Sent from my iPad

Figure 16-14

3. If you need to make changes to the subject or message, tap in either area and make the changes.

4. Tap the Send button and your e-mail is on its way.

You can tap the button with a plus sign on it in the top-right corner of the e-mail message form to display your contacts list and choose recipients from there. This only works with contacts for which you've entered e-mail addresses. See Chapter 15 for more about using the Contacts app.

To cancel an e-mail message and return to Notes without sending it, tap the Cancel button in the e-mail form and then tap Don't Save in the menu that appears. To leave a message but save a draft so you can finish and send it later, tap Cancel and then tap Save. The next time you tap the e-mail button with the same note displayed in Notes, your draft appears.

Delete Notes

1. No sense letting your Notes list get cluttered up, making it harder to find the ones you need. When you're done

with a note, it's time to delete it. Tap the Notes app icon
on the Home screen to open it.

2. With the iPad in landscape orientation, tap on a note in
the notes list to open it.

3. Tap the Trash Can button shown in **Figure 16-15**.

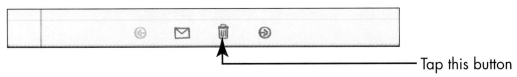

Tap this button

Figure 16-15

4. Tap the Delete Note button that appears (see **Figure
16-16**). The note is deleted.

Tap this button

Figure 16-16

 Notes is a nice little application, but it's limited. It
doesn't offer formatting tools or a way to print the
content you enter without a third-party printing app
like PrinterShare. You can't paste pictures into it (you
can, but what appears is the file name, not the image).
So, if you've made some notes and want to graduate to
building a more robust document in a word processor,
you have a couple of options. One way is to buy the
Pages word processor application for iPad, which costs
about $9.99, and copy your note (using the copy/paste
feature discussed earlier in this chapter). Alternately,
you can send the note to yourself in an e-mail. Open
the e-mail and copy and paste the text into a full-
fledged word processor, and you're good to go.

Troubleshooting and Maintenance

*i*Pads don't grow on trees — they cost a pretty penny. That's why it's important that you learn how to take care of your iPad and troubleshoot any problems that might come up so you get the most out of it.

In this final chapter, I provide some advice about care and maintenance of your iPad, as well as some tips about how to solve common problems, update iPad system software, and even reset iPad should something go seriously wrong.

Keep the iPad Screen Clean

If you've been playing with your iPad at all, you know, despite Apple's claim that iPads have fingerprint-resistant screens, that iPads are fingerprint magnets. Here are some tips about how to clean your iPad screen:

➡ You can get most fingerprints off with a dry, soft cloth such as the one you use to clean your eyeglasses or a cleaning tissue that is lint- and chemical-free.

⟩ If you want to get the surface even cleaner, you can use a soft cloth that has been slightly dampened. Again, make sure whatever cloth material you use is free of lint.

⟩ Turn off iPad and unplug any cables from it before cleaning the screen with a moistened cloth.

⟩ Avoid getting too much moisture around the edges of the screen where it could seep into the unit.

⟩ Never use any household cleaners on your iPad screen. They can degrade the coating that keeps the screen from absorbing oil from your fingers.

 It definitely *isn't* wise to use pre-moistened lens cleaning tissues to clean your screen. Most of these wipes contain alcohol, which can damage the coating.

Protect Your Gadget with a Case

Your screen isn't the only thing on the iPad that can be damaged, so it isn't a bad idea to get a case for it so you can carry it around the house or around town safely. Besides providing a bit of padding if you should drop the device, a case makes the iPad less slippery in your hands, offering a better grip when working with it.

Several cases came out pretty much the day iPad shipped, and more are showing up all the time. You can choose from the neoprene one offered by Apple at around $39 and those from other manufacturers such as Tuff-Luv (www.Tuff-Luv.com) and MiniSuit Case

Manufacturers (`www.globalsources.com/manufacturers/
Mini-Suit-Case.html`) that come in materials ranging from
leather to silicone (see **Figure 17-1** and **Figure 17-2**).

Figure 17-1

 ←A silicone
"skin" case

Figure 17-2

Cases range in price from a few dollars to $70 or more for leather. Some provide a cover (refer to **Figure 17-1**), and others only protect the back and sides (refer to **Figure 17-2**). If you carry your iPad around much at all, consider a case with a cover to provide better protection for the screen or use a screen overlay such as the one from Zagg (www.Zagg.com).

Get Battery Charging Tips

iPad's much touted 10-hour battery life is a wonderful feature, but there are things you can do to extend that battery life even further. Here are a few tips to consider:

➡ You can judge how much battery life you have left by looking at the Battery icon in the far-right corner of the Status bar at the top of your screen.

➡ Hmm . . . I wonder why, but when connected to a Mac computer, iPad can slowly charge; however, some PC connections slowly drain the battery. Even so, the most effective way to charge your iPad is to plug it into the wall outlet using the Dock Connector to USB Cable and the 10W USB Power Adapter that came with your iPad (see **Figure 17-3**).

➡ The fastest way to charge the iPad is to turn it off while charging it.

➡ Your battery may lose some power if you leave it connected to the USB port on a keyboard.

➡ You can use a dock device available from Apple to charge the iPad while it rests in the dock through the connector on the dock itself (see **Figure 17-4**).

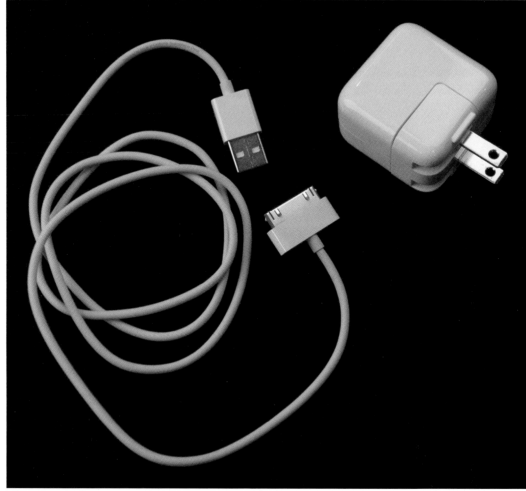

Figure 17-3

 The Battery icon on the Status bar lets you know
   when the charging is complete.

 Your iPad battery is sealed in the unit, so you can't
   replace it as you can with a laptop or cell phone battery. If it's out of warranty, you'll have to fork over
   the money, possibly more than $100 to get a new

battery. See the "Get Support" task, later in this chapter, to find out where to get a replacement battery.

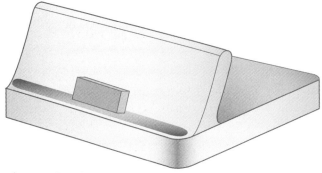

Figure 17-4

Find Out What to Do with a Non-Responsive iPad

If iPad goes dead on you, it's most likely a power issue, so the first thing to do is to plug the Dock Connector to USB Cable into the 10W USB Power Adapter, plug the 10W USB Power Adapter into a wall outlet, plug the other end of the Dock Connector to USB Cable into your iPad, and charge the battery.

Another thing to try — if you think an app is hanging up the iPad — is to press the Sleep/Wake button for a little bit. Next, press and hold the Home key. The app you were using should close.

There's always the old reboot procedure, which in the case of an iPad means pressing the Sleep/Wake button on the top until the red slider is displayed. Drag the slider to turn your iPad off. After a few moments, press the Sleep/Wake button to boot the little guy up again.

If things seem drastic and none of these ideas works, try to reset your iPad. To do this, press the Sleep/Wake button and the Home button together until the Apple logo appears on-screen.

Make the Keyboard Reappear

When you're using a Bluetooth keyboard or the Apple iPad keyboard dock, your on-screen keyboard won't appear. The physical keyboards have, in essence, co-opted keyboard control of your device. Here's what you can do:

⟹ If you're using the iPad Keyboard Dock and want the on-screen keyboard to show up, press the Keyboard button in the set of function buttons that run across the top of the iPad Keyboard Dock. The on-screen keyboard appears.

⟹ To use your on-screen keyboard with a Bluetooth keyboard connected, you have a few options: You can turn the Bluetooth keyboard off, turn off Bluetooth in iPad's General settings, or move the keyboard out of range. Your on-screen keyboard should reappear.

Update Software

1. Apple occasionally updates iPad system software to fix problems or offer enhanced features. It's a good idea to occasionally check for an updated version (say, every month). Start by connecting your iPad to your computer.

2. On your computer, open the iTunes software you installed (see Chapter 3 for more about this).

3. Click on your iPad in the iTunes source list on the left.

4. Click the Summary tab shown in **Figure 17-5**.

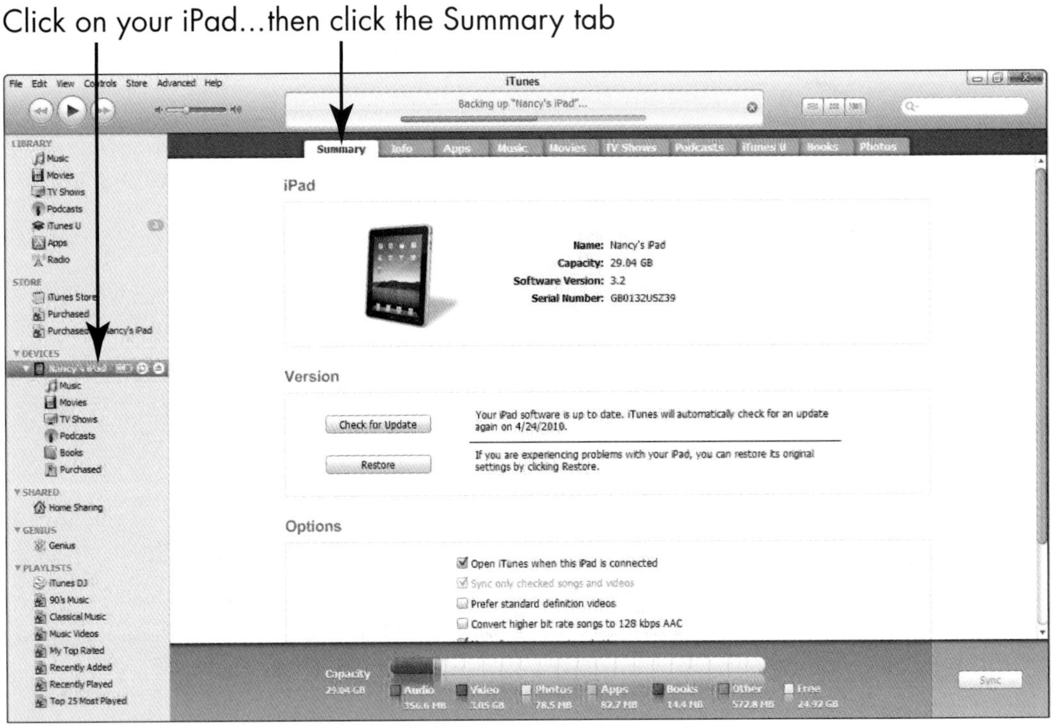

Click on your iPad...then click the Summary tab

Figure 17-5

5. Click the Check for Update button. iTunes displays a message telling you if a new update is available.

6. Click the Update button to install the newest version.

> If you're having problems with iPad, it's possible to use the Update feature to restore the current version of the software on it as a possible fix. Follow the steps above, and then click the Restore button instead of the Update button in Step 6.

Get Sound Back On

Ironically, the very morning I wrote this chapter, my husband was puttering with our iPad. Suddenly, the sound stopped. We gave ourselves a quick course in recovering sound, so now I can share these tips with you:

⟶ If you're using the iPad Keyboard Dock, check to see that you haven't touched the volume control keys on the right side of the top row and inadvertently muted the sound (see **Figure 17-6**).

⟶ Make sure you haven't covered up the speaker in a way that muffles the sound.

⟶ Do you have a headset plugged in? Sound won't play through the speaker and headset at the same time.

⟶ There is a volume limit you can set up in Settings for iPod that will control how loudly iPod can play (useful if you have a teenager around). Tap the Settings icon on the Home screen, then on the left side of the screen that displays, tap iPod and use the Volume Limit controls (see **Figure 17-7**) to make sure Volume Limit is set to Off.

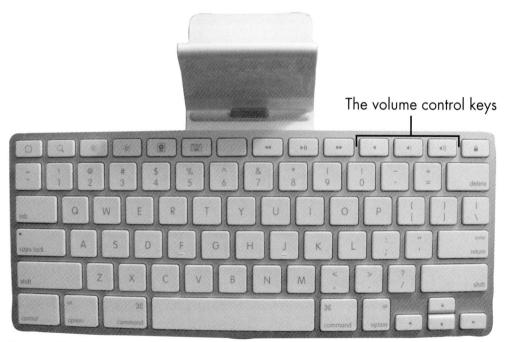

The volume control keys

Figure 17-6

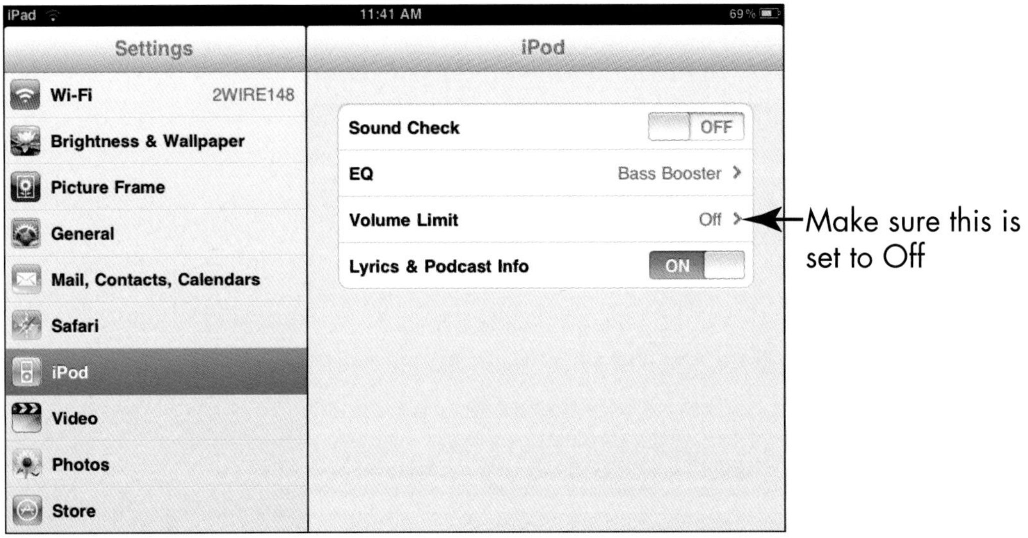

Make sure this is set to Off

Figure 17-7

➠ If all else fails, reboot. That's what worked for us — just press the Sleep/Wake button until the red slider appears. Press and drag the slider to the right. After iPad turns off, press the Sleep/Wake button until the Apple logo appears and you may find yourself back in business sound-wise.

Get Support

Apple is known for its great customer support, so if you're stuck, I definitely recommend you try them out. Here are a few options you can explore for getting help:

➠ Go to your local Apple Store if one is handy and see what the folks there might know about your problem.

➠ Visit the Apple support Web site at www.apple. com/support/ipad (see **Figure 17-8**). Here you'll find online manuals, discussion forums, downloads, and the Apple Expert feature, which enables you to contact a live expert over the phone.

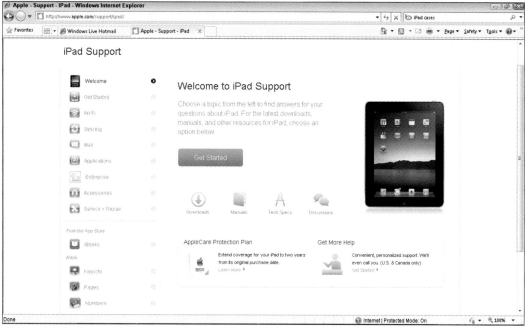

Figure 17-8

⟶ Visit the iPad User Guide at `http://manuals. info.apple.com/en_US/iPad_User_Guide. pdf`. This is a more robust version of the user guide that came with your iPad that you can open using the bookmarked manual on the Safari browser.

⟶ Finally, if you need repair or service for your battery, visit the battery replacement service at `www.apple. com/batteries/replacements.html`.

 Note that Apple recommends that the iPad battery should be replaced only by an Apple Authorized Service Provider.

 **Index**

Podcasts button, iPod Library, 163
Podcasts tab, iTunes, 55
POP3 e-mail account, 100–101
portrait orientation, 102, 148, 274
power adapter, 46
Practice VoiceOver Gestures
     button, 70
pre-installed apps, 134
Press and hold method, 28
previewing in iTunes, 119–121
Previous button
  App Store, 132–133
  iPod app, 167
  Notes app, 279
  Safari, 82
price. *See* cost
Price button, iBookstore, 146–147
Price Grabber for iPad app, 130
PrinterShare, 285
protective case, 288–290
Provide a Payment Method screen,
     iTunes, 50
public WI-FI networks, 81
Purchased button
  iBookstore, 143–144
  iPod Library, 163
purchasing iPad. *See* buying iPad
pushing
  calendar events, 248
  e-mail, 104

• R •

rating YouTube video, 200–201
rebooting, 292, 296
Recent tab, Maps app, 214
Redeem button, iTunes, 123
registering iPad, 21–22

Related tab, YouTube app, 195
Repeat Event dialog, 242
repeating calendar events, 241–242
Reply to option, e-mail, 104–106
Results dialog, Calendar app, 245
Return button, 31
rotating screen feature, 25

• S •

Safari
  adding and using Bookmarks,
     90–92
  adding Web Clips to Home screen,
     92–93
  connecting to Internet, 80–81
  defined, 36
  displaying Web pages as
     thumbnails, 87–89
  exploring, 81–84
  mailing links, 94–95
  navigating Web pages, 84–86
  saving image to photo library, 94
  searching Web, 89–90
  viewing browsing history, 86–87
Satellite view, Maps app, 209, 212
Save Image command, 29
Saved Photos album, 174
saving
  image to photo library, 94
  photos from Web, 173–174
schedule, Calendar app, 236–239
screen. *See also* Home screen
  keeping clean, 287–288
  multi-touch, 22–25
  overlay, 290
  protector, 62
Screen Rotation Lock, 17–18